135837

S0-BEC-389

BF
431
.I 526

WITHDRAWN

Intelligence:
Alternative Views of a Paradigm

Editor: KLAUS F. RIEGEL, Ann Arbor, Mich.

19 73

BIP-87

S. Karger · Basel · München · Paris · London · New York · Sydney

GOSHEN COLLEGE LIBRARY
GOSHEN, INDIANA

Originally published in
Human Development, Vol. 16, No. 1–2 (1973)

S. Karger · Basel · München · Paris · London · New York · Sydney
Arnold-Böcklin-Strasse 25, CH–4011 Basel (Switzerland)

All rights, including that of translation into other languages, reserved.
Photomechanic reproduction (photocopy, microcopy) of this book or parts thereof without
special permission of the publishers is prohibited.

©

Copyright 1973 by S. Karger AG, Verlag für Medizin und Naturwissenschaften, Basel
Printed in Switzerland by Buchdruckerei Gasser & Cie. AG, Basel
ISBN 3-8055-1710-6

Contents

Human Develop. *16:* 1–7 (1973)

An Epitaph for a Paradigm

Introduction for a Symposium

K. F. RIEGEL

University of Michigan, Ann Arbor, Mich.

The young man entered St. Aloysius Roman Catholic church on the campus of Gonzaga University here, carrying a 0.22-caliber rifle and a sledge hammer.

After doing thousands of dollars damage to statues and old Italian marble altars with the sledge hammer, he shot and killed Hilary M. Kunz, a 69-year-old caretaker.

Larry left the church and fired the rifle in several directions. Michael J. Clark, 18, suffered a serious wound in the back. Less seriously wounded were Robert D. Schroeder, 17, Robert A. Fees, 63, and Thomas C. Brass, 24.

Young Harmon died a few feet from the church after being shot by police.

Larry's teachers later said he was the brightest mathematics student ever to attend high schools here. His father, a prominent attorney who considered Larry to be a budding nuclear physicist, said the youth had scored a perfect 100 points in the math portion of a nationwide preuniversity exam and finished in the top one-half of one per cent nationally in the over-all intelligence test.

Newspaper Report, The Ann Arbor News

The underlying epistemological basis of science has profoundly changed during the history of the Western world. In the prescientific period, a firm belief in a supernatural being safeguarded the acquisition of knowledge. While exploring the power of rational thinking, DESCARTES still relied on God to prevent any ill-scheming demon from potentially interfering with our sensory experience. For LOCKE the reliance on sensory information became predominant. Thereby nature took over the roles of the supernatural which, stripped of its anthropomorphic character, was regarded as harmonic and lawful. The scientists' task consisted in 'detecting' the harmonics of the universe (KEPLER) or the laws of nature (NEWTON). New changes were provoked when KANT put these harmonic forms and laws back into the human mind rather than leaving them outside in the metaphysically conceived nature. Farther reaching modifications occurred toward the end of the 19th century when classical natural sciences were extended into their modern complements.

Unfortunately, the behavioral and social sciences, which emerged at about the same time as the reexamination of the natural sciences was proceeding, remained unaffected by these conceptual changes. This conservatism is revealed by their continued uncritical reliance on early viewpoints, especially those of LOCKE and HUME, which became so dogmatic that inquiries into the epistemological basis of the behavioral sciences came to be outrightly rejected as mere philosophical speculations. Raw nature became the sole basis of inquiries to be empirically stripped of its laws through the ceaseless accumulation of data from experiments and testing.

Such naive philosophical realism continued to characterize the thinking of most psychologists. It provoked the blind search for facts and the senseless testing of victims. Its technology cut as crudely as a machete into the jungle which they declared to be our mind and into the chaos which they consider to be our social order. The accumulated results are conglomerates of nonsense syllables and test scores whipped together by the phrase that 'intelligence is what the intelligence tests measure' or, translated to the context of our discussion, 'real is what the intelligence tests measure'. Recently, this naive view of the world and science has been expressed by a well known psychologist, as follows: 'I don't see why people should be disturbed by unequal representation of different groups in different occupations or educationally, *if* it should be found that there are real differences' [cf., NEARY, 1970].

As the behavioral sciences continued on their myriadic path, modern natural sciences engaged in a deep reexamination of their philosophical foundation. As cogently explored by GIORGI [1969], all of the famous scientists, EINSTEIN, BOHR, PLANCK, HEISENBERG, SCHRÖDINGER and many others, participated in this effort. The old rigidified world with its fixed order and determination was contrasted by a pulsing universe which could be interpreted from several different perspectives at the same time [COHEN, 1972]. The material structures were supplemented by systems of energies, and static mechanisms by dynamic processes. While, thereby, any escape from ambiguities and contradictions would seem to lead irreversibly toward abstract formalism, the dialecticism, rediscovered and implemented in modern natural sciences [WUNDT, 1949], led, at the same time, to a renewed appreciation of the human being as the center of our knowledge and understanding.

These major paradigmatic shifts bypassed the behavioral sciences in general and developmental psychology in particular. Psychological gerontologists, being often intellectually far ahead of their colleagues in childhood and adolescence, explored at least a few implications of these modern views of man and society.

Early in the thirties, LORGE [1936] carried convincingly the infamous statement that 'intelligence is what the intelligence test measures' to its logical conclusion. He demonstrated that such a test, when specifically designed for old people, would test the intelligence of old people, would, therefore, show a continuing rise in scores with age and would make many young examinees appear as inferior. Only nowadays, and only as a result of massive social pressure, do students of individual differences admit that tests designed for Woman, Chicanos or Blacks are likely to place the other groups into inferior positions.

LORGE's investigations implied the dependency of psychological evaluations upon the sociocultural preferences under which they are obtained but they did not imply a consideration of historical changes in these conditions. Recent studies in life-span developmental psychology [BALTES, 1968; SCHAIE, 1965], related to similar explorations in the sociology of generational shifts [BENGSTON and BLACK, 1973; RILEY et al., 1972; RYDER, 1965], have led to the explication of the confounded changes in the individual and in society. In contrast, the paradigm traditionally applied in child psychology pretends that individuals grow up in an immobile sociocultural world if not in a sociocultural vacuum. Growth of the individual, as depicted by all the tables and curves in articles and textbooks, is likely to be a mere artifact generated by the systematic disregard of historical changes in education, communication, welfare, etc. [RIEGEL and RIEGEL, 1972]. Except for a sudden decrease in functioning shortly before death (terminal drop), psychological performance during adulthood, for example, does not seem to change at all. Apparent changes may be generated, however, by the increase in mortality with age (and, therefore, by the increasing number of terminal drops) or changes may be produced by generational shifts which are sociological and historical in nature.

The elaboration of developmental research designs, which allow for the unconfounding of the confounded changes in the individual and in society, have tended to emphasize formalistic aspects at the expense of critical evaluations of the changing roles of man and society. The explorations of the sociocultural dependencies of tests have directed our attention toward studies of cultural-historical differences of which our psychological investigations are reflections as much as they contribute to perpetuate these conditions.

Already during the 18th and early 19th centuries two trends in social philosophy and education began to emerge, one of which we have called its 'capitalistic' and the other its 'mercantilistic' branch [RIEGEL, 1972b]. The first dominated in the entrepreneurial socioeconomic systems of England and the United States. Here, development was seen as the outcome of ceaseless competition by which bits and pieces of skills and habits are acquired. The more an individual has accumulated, the better it is for his intellectual and social status. With the white young adult male serving as the exclusive standard of comparison, the very young and old, the deprived and subjugated were bound to be regarded as inferior. Development originated from a fight of everyone against everyone (HOBBES, DARWIN); growth was regarded as the channeling (socialization) of competitive forces into socially acceptable arrangements [ROSENWALD, 1973]; the driving principle was the need for achievement of the 'psychology of more' [LOOFT, 1971] with little or no consideration for structural organization [RIEGEL, 1973b]. The general intelligence test became the prototype for this form of thinking and the standard device for evaluations.

The alternative view of man, society and development emerged under the stratified sociopolitical conditions on the European continent where central administrative and economic control outweighed ceaseless competition. Here, development came to be seen as a stepwise progression through qualitative stages consisting of spontaneous reorganizations of the individual's intellect (PIAGET) and personality (ERIKSON). The young child was seen as basically good, civilization as a cloak which spoils his innocence and beauty (ROUSSEAU). Competition was conceivable within but not between stages. Education emphasized a stage-appropriate approach: a child was to be appreciated and educated as a child (FRÖBEL), an adolescent as an adolescent (PESTALOZZI), and an aged person as an aged person. Moreover, this view of man and his development was open to multigenerational and multicultural variations [RIEGEL, 1972a].

With two basically irreconcilable paradigms thus available, it is little wonder that the recent fury about innateness and subcultural differences in intellectual performance became unreasonable and shortsighted. In spite of their good intentions, most opponents of the innateness thesis continued to operate within the 'capitalistic' paradigm, and thus strengthened the opposed views by reinforcing the conception of man as a competitive beast directed by the 'psychology of more'. All that these scholars could achieve was to reject a few minor inconsistencies and errors in the nativists' research and interpretations. On the other hand, those opponents committed to the 'mercantilistic' paradigm were more profound in their criticism but, by rejecting the 'capitalistic' viewpoint of man and development, they argued in a scientific language which was incompatible with that of their opponents to whom it appeared, therefore, as loose, superficial and irrelevant. Moreover, like their opponents, they failed to consider the dependency of the individual's development on sociocultural conditions and changes. As pointedly emphasized by WILDEN [1972], their developmental psychology explicated an ideal state of the mind and, thus, an alienated structure of 'law and order'. They did not provide insights and instructions on how these structures can be attained by persons who do not know them, and they fail to give aid and comfort to those who suffer by being deprived of them.

As implied in our criticism, several different paradigms of man, society and their development are conceivable [LOYE, 1971]. A choice among them is not dependent upon the detection of a 'true' or 'real' development in a metaphysically conceived nature but upon our constructive and emancipatory efforts to generate a psychological model which accounts for the dialectic transformations of the projective biological and the introjective cultural-historical developments [RIEGEL, 1973a]. The 'truth' of such a model can only lie in the consistency of the biological, individual, and societal transformations, but not in external (including material) criteria. Such a developmental-historical conception coincides with, or rather has been prepared by, the theories of modern natural sciences.

In order to achieve such extensions, the 'mercantilistic' paradigm needs to take account of the social structures and transformations through which this paradigm itself has emerged. Presently, it may account for the intrinsic interactions between biological and psychological forces and, in this regard, can neither be regarded as simply nativistic or environmentalistic. However, we also need to comprehend development as a process of social interactions, which from the outside transforms the organism as he transforms the external conditions through his own activities. In comparison to this model (elaborated most clearly in cognitive developmental psychology) the 'capitalistic' paradigm (representing conceptually the 'psychology of more' and technologically the general intelligence test) can only serve as a demonstration of the failure of a naive, though harmful, conception of man, society and their development. It can continue to serve in an antithetical manner, but it is dead as a constructive force on its own.

The following collection of treatises aims at contributing to the efforts of laying this body to rest. None of these contributions criticizes particular shortcomings and errors of the old paradigm. They rather elaborate alternatives or critical issues that make these viewpoints diametrically distinct from the old paradigm. In this effort, they cut across several interrelated dimensions.

FISCHER promotes a phenomenological approach to psychological development; FURTH rejects the nature-nurture controversy from a Piagetian point of view; LEWIS proposes an interaction model of early development; OVERTON questions the additivity assumption of developmental conceptions; WOHLWILL explores the concept of experience from an ecological point of view; ELIAS elaborates sociocultural implications and directions of behavior genetics.

Several contributions engage in cross-cultural and historical comparisons: LOOFT explores issues of social philosophy and educational influences; TULKIN and KONNER analyze the cultural relativity of intellectual functions; WOZNIAK compares the conception of intellectual development dominant in the West with that promoted in the Soviet Union; WEINER contrasts developmental progression in regard to achievement success and moral efforts.

The present author does not share all of the viewpoints expressed in these treatises, nor does he expect that these authors share all of the viewpoints expressed by the writer of this epitaph, but he fully supports the authors' efforts to call attention to or to provide alternative conceptions of man, society and their development. The old paradigm, according to which man is engaged in a continuous, selfish struggle for his advancement, more in the material than in the intellectual or moral sense, is dead. Perhaps it continues to serve a useful function by demonstrating its insufficiencies and by helping us to recognize more clearly the directions of our renewed efforts. The contributions included in this collection have parted company with the old paradigm, but an advanced synthesis might still have to come, a synthesis in which man is not merely a passive receptacle within a passive world but in which the individual through his own efforts transforms the world while, at the same time, being transformed himself.

References

BALTES, P.B.: Longitudinal and cross-sectional sequences in the study of age and generation effects. Human Develop. *11:* 145–171 (1968).

BENGSTON, V.L. and BLACK, K.D.: Inter-generational relations and continuities in socialization; in BALTES and SCHAIE Life-span developmental psychology: personality and socialization (in press, Academic Press, New York 1973).

COHEN, D.: Time as energy. On the application of modern concepts of time to developmental sciences; unpublished manuscript (Univ. of Southern California, Los Angeles 1972).

GIORGI, A.: Psychology. A human science. Soc. Res. 36: 412–432 (1969).

LOOFT, W.R.: The psychology of more. Amer. Psychol. 26: 561–565 (1971).

LORGE, I.: The influence of the test upon the nature of mental decline as a function of age. J. educ. Psychol. 27: 100–110 (1936).

LOYE, D.E.: The healing of a nation (Norton, New York 1971).

NEARY, J.: A scientist's variation on a disturbing racial theme. Life 68: 64 (1970).

RIEGEL, K.F.: Developmental psychology and society. Some historical and ethical considerations; in NESSELROADE and REESE Life-span developmental psychology: methodological issues, pp. 1–23 (Academic Press, New York 1972a).

RIEGEL, K.F.: The influence of economic and political ideologies upon the development of developmental psychology. Psychol. Bull. 78: 129–141 (1972b).

RIEGEL, K.F.: Dialectic operations. The final period of cognitive development. Human Develop. (in press, 1973a).

RIEGEL, K.F. (ed.): Structure, transformation, interaction. Developmental and historical aspects. Topics in Human Develop., vol. 1 (in press, Karger, Basel 1973b).

RIEGEL, K.F. and RIEGEL, R.M.: Development, drop, and death. Develop. Psychol. 6: 306–319 (1972)

RILEY, M.W.; JOHNSON, W., and FONER, A. (eds.): Aging and society. A sociology of age stratification, vol. 3 (Russell Sage Foundation, New York 1972).

ROSENWALD, G.: Self, group, and society. An interactionist critique; in RIEGEL Structure, transformation, interaction: developmental and historical aspects. Topics in Human Develop., vol. 1 (in press, Karger, Basel 1973).

RYDER, N.B.: The cohort as a concept in the study of social changes. Amer. Soc. Rev. 30: 843–861 (1965).

SCHAIE, K.W.: A general model for the study of developmental problems. Psychol. Bull. 64: 92–108 (1965).

WILDEN, A.: System and structure. Essays in communication and exchange (Tavistock, London 1972).

WUNDT, M.: Hegels Logik und die moderne Physik (Westdeutscher Verlag, Köln 1949)

Request reprints from: Dr. KLAUS F. RIEGEL, Educational Testing Service, *Princeton, NJ 08540* (USA)

Human Develop. *16:* 8–20 (1973)

Intelligence contra IQ

A Human Science Critique and Alternative to the Natural Science Approach to Man

Constance T. Fischer

Duquesne University, Pittsburgh, Pa.

Abstract. With the transformation of intelligence into IQ as a concrete reference point, this article indicates the general social impact of psychology practiced as a natural science. A metascience examiniation of the latter's approach to man reveals the interrelations of its assumptions, methods, and content, while thus suggesting the need for a specifically human science. This alternative's assumptions, methods, and content are specified as being rooted in a rigorous existential-phenomenological philosophy. The human science approach is proffered as one comprehensive enough to account for man's possibilities as well as his necessary restrictions. A human science understanding of intelligence is presented, along with remarks about its practical implementation.

Key Words
Intelligence
IQ
Human science
Metascience
Scientism
Educational goals
Psychological testing
Existential psychology
Phenomenological psychology

This paper first briefly overviews the prevailing psychological paradigm, that of psychology conceived as a pre-Heisenberg natural science. Specifically, the interrelations of its assumptions, methods, and content are pointed out. Then some of its general negative social consequences are summarized, followed by specific mention of its consequences for conceptions of intelligence. The assumptions, methods, and content of a specifically human science paradigm then are presented. This section is followed by a human science discussion of the meaning of intelligence. The paper closes with a few remarks about implementation of a human science approach to intelligence.

Critique of the Natural Science Approach to Human Phenomena

Midnineteenth century found European intellectuals celebrating man's increasing participation in his own destiny. They were certain not only that the natural world was orderly, but that as partially an object of nature, man too was orderly. Above all, his relationship to nature could be discovered, comprehended, and utilized by man. In England, the Lockean tradition of philosophical empiricism nurtured efforts to discover the laws underlying phenomena as widespread as the influence of events on mental associations to genetic influence on ear shape. Efforts to evaluate the effectiveness of experimentation in agriculture yielded statistical procedures for all empirical fields. In France, DESCARTES' tradition of mind-body split and interaction, enhanced by the Lockean *tabula rasa* notions, supported efforts to liberate man by providing appropriate environments for the children of the Revolution, for PINEL's insane, ITARD's feral child, and BINET's public school children. In Germany, these thrusts were located primarily in the work of such physicists and physiologists as FECHNER and HELMHOLTZ, who sought to apply existing methods of natural science to the presumed interactions between the mental and the physical. The ensuing psychophysical methods, which sought to discover universal laws, evolved into *the* method for psychology, determining its content in the process.

In retrospect, we now can see that the initial threefold interest in man as a participant in his destiny, as a seeker of greater freedom, and as a unique phenomenon traveling through nature, was subverted by the accompanying interest in the natural world. In effect, psychology became a natural science, and man became strictly an object of nature. Psychology assumed that its business was to uncover the universal laws operating out in nature, independent of man. Hence, it also assumed that its work was independent of values and of philosophy. Psychology's 'philosophy of science' was automatically equated with nineteenth century logical empiricism and positivism. Now, however, a broader philosophy of science, known through studies of metascience, is examining the assumptions underlying varying approaches to human phenomena – from the natural scientific to the social/humanistic [e.g., RADNITZKY, 1970; GRAUMANN, 1970]. These and related analyses [GIORGI, 1970] demonstrate the interdependence of approach, method, and content.

The assumptions of the pre-Heisenberg natural science approach are that reality is separate from and independent of observation, and that man too is an object of nature. Reality is ordered in a mathematical, logical (Aristotelian) manner, amenable to classification. All events are explained ultimately in terms of physical causation – absolute determinism, although the (quantitative) characteristics of the (isolatable) variables do interact. These interactions are describable via mathematical equations. In short, the natural science approach to man is that of scientistism – the assumption that all science must be modeled after the pre-Heisenberg physical sciences. In addition to these standard, explicit assertions from the early field of natural science, there are two usually unacknowledged guiding interests or concerns [HABERMAS, 1966] – those of attaining certainty and of controlling or directing the process of nature.

The methods of natural science are, then, objective observation, quantitative measurement, analysis into parts and interactions, and controlled experimentation. The latter takes the form of establishing particular conditions and measuring the success of the experimental operations. The resulting data are presumed to represent absolutely determined reactions to identical repetitions of procedure. Further, these data are regarded not as constituted through a prior organization of our experience, in terms of instrumental action and function, but as 'givens' – isolatable, immutable, unequivocal facts about an external reality. Through this paradigm experimentation necessarily hypostatizes its observations. Finally, in its search for certainty about universal order, natural scientific psychology transforms the person's individualness into a statistical location on a predetermined dimension. Thus, the content of the field of 'individual differences' is in actuality tables of mass data indexed in terms of standard deviations, correlation coefficients, etc. They address neither the individual nor difference *per se*.

The general limitation of applying this natural science to man is that it fails to account for the scientist's co-constitution of his science. More specifically, scientistic psychology can study man only in the third person; it cannot address the (first person) experimenter himself. Put still differently, it cannot account for the possibility of the experimenter manipulating nature. Indeed, natural science can account only for the realm of the necessary. It has no way to approach the realm of the possible, let alone that interface between necessity and possibility, between man's subjectness and subjectedness, which is the subjectmatter of a human scientific psychology. These limitations bear heavy social consequences.

Social Consequences of Imposing Scientistic Order on Human Phenomena

In General

The view that scientists merely uncover unequivocal, immutable facts leaves its believers resigned to adapt to the laws of nature. This view minimizes efforts to alter existing situations. Thus, the scientistic approach to man tends to serve the *status quo,* as often as not thereby also perpetuating unwitting as well as motivated oppression. The obvious example here is the conclusion that blacks should be channeled into jobs requiring only rote memory skills since standardized tests have shown blacks to be inferior in abstract thinking.

The above example also illustrates another consequence of the scientistic approach: Its conclusions are assumed to be somehow purely scientific – untainted by moral, philosophical, political, economic, or other involvement or implication. Scientific findings have been beyond social reproach since facts in themselves are said to be value-free. Similarly, the manner and circumstances in which appearances are apprehended as facts go unquestioned; no effort is made to examine human participation in what it *takes* as 'given'.

In like manner, whatever is not amenable to the scientist's existing methods of measurement is regarded as not real. If it is not directly observable or quantifiable through its products, it isn't. Disputation is limited to existing scientistic variables. Where science has not 'worked', the solution is sought in still more of the same sort of data. The natural science psychologist is locked into one system; other persons, views, and phenomena are locked out.

Since it is assumed that only science uncovers valid reality, scientists have become an elite group, with power over the destiny of those who march to different drums. Applications for government grants, manuscripts, doctoral examinations must all be presented in accordance with the scientistic paradigm. Further, this paradigm requires terminology so far removed from the everyday life from which it was derived, that only the elite can speak their technologized language. Hence, most 'factual' research reports are mystifying to the public. Indeed, the subject of a psychological or educational evaluation frequently is not allowed access to his own records, on the grounds that he wouldn't understand them anyway. Besides, it is said, he might not be able to cope with the ultimate truth to which his life has been reduced. Thus, the person is doubly subjected to being treated as the product of forces and traits beyond his comprehension as well as to secrecy from him among the powerful elite. Initiative and self-responsibility thus are systematically undermined.

This undermining of initiative is also a consequence of the scientistic penchant for categorizing persons into presumably distinct classes, according to 'given' traits. Here a dual assumption is operative: (a) A person either has or doesn't have the trait or 'enough' of it; (b) 'it' must be stimulated from outside to become operative, hence necessitating placement by quantity of 'it' into various categories of environment. Further, not only does this categorizing thus fulfill its own prediction of level of achievement, it also fosters a divisive society. People frequently see themselves in terms of 'us' and 'them', groups with immutable, 'given', differences. Change is seen in terms of reaction to force. The only conception of dialectics is of the antithetical sort; external categorization of 'givens' does not lend itself to a sense of mutuality of person and world (or other person). Scientistic psychology thus impedes true community. We have no psychology of dialectical process, of growth through mutual evolution, of social possibility. We have instead a psychology of determinism and control, which in effect subverts hope, initiative, and dialogue.

In Regard to Intelligence

Psychology has no established literature on intelligence. That nineteenth century laboratory interest in psychophysical relations evolved into an elaborate quantitative methodology that *produced* psychology's content. Scientistic psychology has failed to take human phenomena in their own right first, and then attempt to develop methods appropriate to them. Our current scientific literature, then, is about IQ, not intelligence. IQ is an artifact of the psychometric movement. It is also intimately related to Western public school criteria of educational success, which were explicitly built into the first intelligence test at the turn of the century by BINET. Specifically, IQ-test items are aimed at exposure to (a) predetermined and single perspective truth, (b) memorization of facts-as-facts, and (c) application of presented facts to logical problem-solving. In actuality, IQ-tests test for level of school achievement; but IQ is then regarded as what underlies that achievement. IQ is seen as the core of intelligent being, as necessary for, and determinative of, success. This circular reduction not only keeps the low scorer down, it is also oppressive to society in general. Specifically, it gives scientific recognition and approval to only one kind of intelligence: the one-truth/analytic perspective. Competence in other approaches equally necessary for the survival of high quality society are not adequately recognized, rewarded, or promoted. Examples: respect for truth as perspectival, aesthetic comprehension, sense of community, capacity for awe, interpersonal sensitivity, initiative and self-responsibility, atunement to transition, joyful participation, etc. In short, the reduction of intelligence to IQ imposes limited and limiting values on all those who are subject to professional influence, whether as students, job applicants, or patients.

Even where controversies about intelligence arise, they have been argued primarily within the IQ paradigm. The *current* question of racial inferiority could be posed only within a system of hypostacized, isolated, measured, presumably interacting, traits. Only where man is wrenched apart into such quasi-natural forces [HABERMAS, 1966] could intelligence be said to consist of '80%' genetic factors. Similarly, questions of IQ constancy as well as of general versus specific factors of IQ could arise only where the research conditions are restrictively controlled, where items are preselected along a limited dimension, and where achievement is staticized. Efforts to correct the abuses of the psychometric tradition must aim at its foundations, not its content. For example, blacks will not improve their situation by continuing to demand black norms and testers for standardized IQ-tests. They are condemned to being judged as deficient as a group by virtue of being different, until efforts are made to study difference qualitatively.

Finally, the reduction of intelligence to IQ has discouraged efforts to attend to the individual person. The school child, for example, is programmed and evaluated primarily against an actuarial 'average' person of his own age. The criterion of both academic potential and success is 'how much' rather than 'what/when/how'. Further, the focus on 'how much' limits attention to the past – as already given potential or as already scored achievement. The individual's active participation, his *moving toward* accomplishment, goes unattended. Likewise, except as objectified stimulus variables, the person's situation as he lives it is lost. Thus, we lose the opportunity to study the relations between person and surrounding institutions in specific, and in general the relation between necessity and possibility, between what must be accepted and what man can hope to alter.

Even such a cursory critique as the above can serve to liberate us from the automatic practice and consequences of applying natural science assumptions and methods to human phenomena. But critique is not adequate; an alternative approach must be attempted.

A Human Science Approach

In General

GIORGI [1970] has introduced the title 'psychology as a human science' to indicate an explicit alternative to the traditional practice of natural science psychology. This alternative approach attempts to accept man in his own right, as more than an object of nature, and *then* to develop research methods that are specifically appropriate to him. This human science approach is, then, an existential-phenomenological psychology. It is concerned with existential man – who behaves in accordance with his participative experience of situations. The unit of study is the relational unity of person and world, man-in-his-world, rather than man affecting world or world affecting man. When we look to our everyday lives, we find that man is always intentional – not just in the sense of being purposive, but also in BRENTANO'S sense of always intending some*thing,* of always being in tune with a perceived world. While person and world are certainly distinguishable, in this sense they are not separable. Similarly, for man there can be no world except that as known by man; he co-constitutes his own observations. There are no facts except those apprehended by man in his own way. Natural science is a construction derived from this lived world. [See SARTRE, 1956, 1963, as primary references to existential themes, or STRASSER, 1963, as a secondary source.]

It is the method of psychology as a human science that is phenomenological. Here this term does not refer to introspectionism nor to mere acknowledgement of the importance of individual experience. The phenomenology referred to at present is in the philosophical tradition of HUSSERL [1931] and HEIDEGGER [1962]; see ZANER [1970] or GELVEN [1970] as secondary sources.

In the psychological endeavor, however, there is no attempt to attain a presuppositionless position nor to pursue HUSSERL'S transcendental reduction. And while human science psychology is indebted to the ontological work of phenomenology, its own effort is directed toward describing universal structures of embodied existence. The works of MERLEAU-PONTY [e.g. 1963, 1968] have been seminal for this project.

More specifically, the human science method is directed toward apprehending phenomena *as they appear* prior to theoretical interpretation. The method, then, is a dialectical one – an effort to understand and to appreciate the already-there lived perceptions on the part of self and others, through dialogue between researcher and researched. In this dialogue there are mutual implications and influences between the method and its subject as well as within the dynamic past-present-future. The goal is to describe the phenomenon not with instrumental or other final precision, but so that it becomes transparent – recognizable through its varied manifestations in various contexts. Just such definition of the phenomenon should precede any of the more traditional research in which the phenomenon is regarded as a factor, or even as a variable. Research procedures include review of the literature, and reflection on one's own experiences, as well as on instances one encounters in everyday life. Then a more formal and easily sharable procedure can be the collection of recorded reports from research subjects. The common phenomenal characteristics can be drawn out and presented in an integrated form as the phenomenal structure – the phenomenon as immediately experienced. Upon further reflection, the fuller, fundamental structure can become apparent. The latter effort involves explicitation of the situational and existential preconditions of the phenomenal structure. Always, these descriptions try to be faithful to lived experience, and to avoid reductive interpretation.

An example of a phenomenological structural analysis (of the experience of anger): 'Anger is the prereflective experience of being made unable by an other who prevents us, and it is the counteraction of this sense of inability by an affective transformation of the other and of the relationship with the other. The body is experienced as bursting forth, and expresses itself, publicly or privately as each person's prereflective restrictions allow, in expansive, explosive, nontypical behavior'. [STEVICK, 1971, p. 144; see analyses of anxiety, W.F. FISCHER; privacy, C.T. FISCHER; and learning, P.F. COLAIZZI, in the same volume.]

The above existential-phenomenological psychology *is* scientific. Specifically, its rigor consists in the insistence that its analyses account for every encountered instance of the phenomenon; there are no statistical probability levels. The effort toward transparency continues as further nuances or variations stand out. In addition, the transparency must be evident to all viewers addressing the lived world. It is rigorous also in that it attempts to specify its own assumptions and perspectives, including the active engagement of the researcher. Finally, this human psychology is scientific in that it accounts for phenomena in a sharable, demonstrable, repeatable manner. It does so not by reducing the phenomenon to a different order or by pointing to causes, but by describing *what* the phenomenon is, including the conditions necessary for its occurrence.

Physiological, neurological, etc., conditions are also part of the fuller structure, although so far most phenomenological studies have simply assumed them without investigating how their variations participate in varied phenomenal structures. The core *content* of human science, then, is structural analyses of phenomena as humanly experienced. These structures consist of the mutually implicatory dimensions and preconditions necessary and sufficient to the phenomenon. Similarly, human changes from one state to another are understood as restructurations, as dialectical transformations, rather than as linear reactions.

Note that this human science does not posit an absolute freedom. It simply acknowledges that the meanings of the situations in which man finds himself are co-constituted by him. He participates in the significance to him of restrictions to his forward movement, thus escaping complete determination. Study of this co-constitution and forward thrust, which are admittedly limited by their own structure and situatedness, encourages liberation of hope and action (the 'possible') from those conditions which are only *man*ufactured necessity.

In Regard to Intelligence

Except for the scientized version, 'intelligence' has referred to the variable ways a person is in effective touch with his world. Specifically, 'intelligence' is akin to the layman's sense of 'personality'; both terms point to a person's multiform styles and modes of openness through which he deals with typical, varied, and new phenomena. 'Intelligence', however, points to these approaches more specifically in terms of their effectiveness. While one can make general statements about typical approaches and degrees of accomplishment, in actuality intelligent behavior always occurs in a concrete situation. The productive approach is always to something in particular and always within a specific context. Further, any judgment of effectiveness presupposes valued ends – effectiveness in accomplishing what, toward what further goal? Assumptions about man's nature are always implicit in these values. In short, intelligence is not some*thing* which one *has,* but is instead an interpersonal judgment about the power of the way one does something.

The above human science conception can serve to de-reify intelligence and to expand it beyond the one-truth/analytic value that is embodied in IQ tests. But as yet there are no phenomenological research analyses of various universal ways of moving effectively. To date, most empirical/ reflective analyses have focused on states of being rather than on movement. Analyses of effective approaches, however, would certainly attempt to apprehend their structural unity. That is, they would try to describe their distinguishable dimensions without conceiving of them as separate categories.

For example, I refer to behavior, or experiaction [VON ECKARTSBERG, 1971], as 'moving'. As a means of staying in touch with the latter's complex structure, we can acknowledge the simultaneity of both the 'how' of one's moving, and the 'territory' through which he moves. The 'how' and the 'territory' are, of course, mutually implicatory, as are their components. This 'how' the moving occurs could be abstracted roughly as consisting of *bond* (e.g., openness, being at, guardedness; want, ought, must; can, uncertain, can't), *embodiment* (e.g., sweating, breathing easily) of *mode* (e.g., imagining, reflecting, willing, touching), and *style* (strategies, pathways, sequences). 'Territory' consists of the lived places, objects, persons, and events that one moves through, toward, for whom, from about, and from the face of. Many further distinctions could be made, of course, such as territory as taken for granted, as goal, as obstacle, etc. This general conception is not intended as a grid to be imposed on behavior, but rather as a reminder that human being is not completely object-like. Human being also implies a relational unity with its world. Note, for example, that any given moment of moving could be mapped out in terms of how the person gets through what. However, even the described moving would be understood as being from the perspective of the engaged observer. This mapping describes what the behavior is. No further explanation would be called for. There would be no need to hypothesize affect and intellect as separate and interacting. And effective approaches would not be limited to a purely cognitive realm.

Even when phenomenological analyses of effective moving become available, however, evaluation of individual intelligence would have to be conducted individually. After all, it is the concrete form of the universal structure that must be described if the individual is to be understood and served in his own right. An excerpt from such an individual assessment:

When Irene is familiar with some of the features of a new task, she confidently settles on an overall plan which begins with the familiar points. Then she flits about within the plan, venturing into the new until it too is familiar. For example, when antiquing a desk, she boldly applied paint to some of the broad surfaces, then tentatively dabbed at a drawer knob, went back to complete the top surface, then experimented with the decorative front, and so on to completion. But when confronted with a less familiar task, Irene sits back somewhat apprehensively and awaits assistance, as when she was being taught to produce alpha waves. Or, when nevertheless sure of her ultimate success, she maps out a detailed sequence of steps and self-hints, as when she determinedly wrote out lengthy notes prior to embarking on her first overseas trip.

Within all these variations, Irene ensures that details are completed in such a way that they serve the final product, whether it be an attractive desk, an alpha wave, or an efficient and enjoyable journey. It is when left in unfamiliar, uncertain territory, without supervision, that Irene is least effective.

This partial excerpt can illustrate that all ways of moving get one somewhere, and that inquiry must be made about which further possibilities are both opened and closed by a particular approach. This is the point at which effectiveness is judged, and at which values must be questionned. Moreover, dealing with such concrete events, rather than with test scores, allows concomitant investigation of both inhibitory and facilitative aspects of the person's environment. In addition, intelligence is not wrested from comportment as though it were an independent, determinative, entity. As well as bypassing totalizations or reductions, description of actual behaviors also diminishes esoterica and professional elitism. For example, with this sort of data, there is no need for keeping evaluations secret from the assessee. Finally, description of 'moving' is a reminder that any situation includes both given contingencies and the person's own relation to them. The latter can be a passageway to at least some change, initiated either by self or by other.

Implementation of a Human Science Approach to Intelligence

The practice of psychology as a human science has been proposed here as a corrective to the negative consequences of the natural science approach to man. No doubt, this human science shall prove to have its own limitations; but at least these should occur within a system that recognizes greater potential in man than has natural science psychology. In the meantime, the age of technology and mass media has awakened the populace's sense of multiperspectives, relativity, and of dimensions versus dichotomies, while at the same time exposing the subjective, perspectival, and altogether fallible character of modern expertise and professionalism. We are ready for a science that can take into account man's more-than-object nature.

However, crisis and readiness are not enough. Nor does the availability of an alternative theory and research methodology provide an adequate addition. Consonant language and practices for use in daily life must be provided. And while the theory may be as complex and as guiding as that of established psychology, if it is to be a proper corrective its referents and validity criteria always must be life events as they appear in everyday existence. In addition, bridges must be built between the practices and data of the earlier approach and those of the newer one. For example, I have published a definition of IQ-intelligence with which theorists of varying persuasions can agree [FISCHER, 1969]. It offers clarification of many standard IQ controversies, in addition to opening the way to the sort of conception of intelligence suggested here. Then, in other sources [e.g., 1973] I have presented concrete procedures for clinical and educational assessment, accompanied by actual examples. It is through the work of practitioners that theories have their effects; it will be the introduction of such human science practices that shall occasion dialectical change for both forms of science.

References

FISCHER, C.T.: Intelligence defined as effectiveness of approaches. J. cons. clin. Psychol. *33:* 668–674 (1969).

FISCHER, C.T.: Exit IQ: enter the child; in WILLIAMS and GORDON Clinical child psychology: current practices and future perspectives. (Section on clinical child psychology, Amer. Psychol. Ass., Washington 1973).

GELVEN, M.: A commentary on HEIDEGGER's 'Being and time' (Harper & Row, New York 1970).

GIORGI, A.: Psychology as a human science: a phenomenologically based approach (Harper & Row, New York 1970).

GRAUMANN, C.F.: Conflicting and convergent trends in psychological theory. J. phenomenol. Psychol. *1:* 51–61 (1970).

HABERMAS, J.: Knowledge and interest. Inquiry *9:* 285–300 (1966).

HEIDEGGER, M.: Being and time (Harper & Row, New York 1962).

HUSSERL, E.: Ideas: general introduction to pure phenomenology (Macmillan, New York 1931).

HUSSERL, E.: The crisis of European sciences and transendental philosophy (Northwestern University Press, Evanston 1970).

MERLEAU-PONTY, M.: The structure of behavior (Beacon Press, Boston 1963).

MERLEAU-PONTY, M.: The visible and the invisible (Northwestern University Press, Evanston 1968).

RADNITZKY, G.: Contemporary schools of metascience (Scandinavian University Books, Stockholm 1970).

SARTRE, J.P.: Being and nothingness (Philosophical Library, New York 1956).

SARTRE, J.P.: Search for a method (Knopf, New York 1963).

STEVICK, E.L.: An empirical investigation of the experience of anger; in GIORGI, FISCHER and VON ECKARTSBERG Duquesne studies in phenomenological psychology (Duquesne University Press, Pittsburgh 1971).

STRASSER, S.: Phenomenology and the human sciences (Duquesne University Press, Pittsburgh 1963).

VON ECKARTSBERG, R.: On experiential methodology; in GIORGI, FISCHER and VON ECKARTSBERG Duquesne studies in phenomenological psychology (Duquesne University Press, Pittsburgh 1971).

ZANER, R.M.: The way of phenomenology: criticism as a philosophical discipline (Pegasus, New York 1970).

Request reprints from: Dr. CONSTANCE T. FISCHER, Department of Psychology, Duquesne University, *Pittsburgh, PA 15219* (USA)

Human Develop. *16:* 21–32 (1973)

Conceptions of Human Nature, Educational Practice, and Individual Development

W. R. LOOFT

Pennsylvania State University, University Park, Pa.

Abstract. The continuing debate over the ability/hered-ity/environment issue is a clear manifestation of the under-lying assumptions about human nature that permeate the social economic, and educational institutions of America. It is argued here that this set of assumptions – or model of man – is neither necessary nor desirable for a humane society; that the educational system has been the principal agent in disse-minating this view; that alternative views of society and human nature were available at critical points in the history of the United States, but that economic and war-time conditions were decisive in fostering support for only certain views of human nature; and that alternative, more desirable views are still available, but that only radical action can lead toward any possibility of realizing these alternatives.

Key Words
Ability
Compensatory education
Educational practice
History of education
Intelligence
Model of man
Standardized testing

In a pamphlet entitled 'Criteria for Admission' that was distributed in 1972 by the psychology department of a major American university there appears the following statement regarding the kind of student that is desired for admission into graduate study:

'All other things being equal, we are more interested in those who have already demonstrated that they have intellectual skills and sophistication. ... It occasionally happens that a student with a poor academic record has so impressed his mentor with his research enthusiasm, sophistication and dedication that we can take a chance with him. But this is an exception; the typical student offered admission is one with strong test scores, a good academic record, and whose advisors write that the student is strongly committed to four or five years of full time graduate work and a productive professional career.'

Probably most university professors and administrators and most of the masses of young people who applied for admission to graduate schools during 1972 will find nothing remarkable or offensive in this pronouncement; these persons have either written similar kinds of statements themselves or have encountered them in their own pursuits so often that they naturally assume that this is the proper order of things. The position to be presented in this paper is that this condition is not necessarily the 'proper' order of things at all; it is to be viewed as only one – and indeed an unfortunate one – of many possible orientations regarding merit, individual worth, and societal order.

This graduate department's view of the most desirable kind of student input is yet another manifestation of the set of conditions and attitudes that set off the most recent installment of the persistent controversy over the ability/heredity/environment question. The quoted statement is little more than a rephrasing of the arguments offered by JENSEN [1969], HERRNSTEIN [1971], and others in the current cadre of the inherited-intelligence proponents. What is even more alarming – and ultimately depressing – is that very likely most all of their critics would also find nothing disagreeable in the statement. This fact explains why virtually no progress has been made in our understanding of human ability in the aftermath of the JENSEN controversy. Despite the appearance of plurality and diversity among all the people in the American continent, the society itself is maintained by a conception of human nature that permeates all groups and institutions. This model of man – which may be described, perhaps with limited usefulness, by the appellation the 'Psychology of More' [LOOFT, 1971] – pervades all aspects of society, including government, economics, educational practice, and individuals.

The purpose of this paper is to argue that this set of assumptions is neither necessary nor desirable for a humane society; that the educational system has been the principal agent in disseminating this view; that alternative views of society and human nature were available at critical points in the history of the United States, but that economic and war-time conditions were decisive in fostering support for only certain views of human nature; and that alternative, more desirable views are still available, but that only radical action can lead toward any possibility of realizing these alternatives.

Functions of American Education through History

Another criticism of the American educational system hardly seems necessary; first of all, it would probably make for dull reading, and secondly, this task has been done often and brilliantly by several persons in recent years. Therefore, the purpose of the discussion to follow is to illustrate how certain developments at critical periods in the history of the public school system have directly contributed to the creation of the present controversy and the attendant beliefs regarding human nature.

An apposite form of historical analysis is to ascertain the functions the schools were intended to serve at various periods in the history of this country [cf. PERKINSON, 1968]. In the early beginnings – the pioneer and colonial periods – the settlers on the northeast coast perceived the importance of schools in essentially two ways. First, they served an important baby-sitting function; both parents had to devote their energies to eking out the bare essentials for living, and thus they had little time for child care. Second, parents' Old Testament view of human nature led them to believe that if their children were left untended, they would quickly degenerate into savages, not unlike the 'savages' that already populated the New World. Thus, the compulsory education laws passed in 1642 and 1647 in Massachusetts marked the beginning of a characteristic of American education that persists to the present day: All children must attend school and be exposed to whatever happens therein.

Later in the colonial period a shift in the perceived function of schooling can be discerned. Through its early history America suffered a severe labor shortage, and this situation led to the development of a number of distinct conditions, including the introduction of slaves and the failure to create an apprenticeship system similar to that existing in Europe. Basically, as this was a land of the unexpected, it was up to the schools to prepare the young generation for the unexpected. It was felt that they must learn how to perform many diverse tasks, not just one.

After the Revolution and the gaining of independence from England, Americans came to expect a new function from their schools – a political function. To prevent further government tyranny, it was believed that an educated, intelligent citizenry was needed to make the new republic work. More particularly, as THOMAS JEFFERSON put it, there was a need to create 'a national aristocracy of talent', or a relatively small corps of enlightened leaders to operate the machinery of government and society. This attitude did not prevail long, however, for by the 1820s, with the appearance of the Jacksonian democrats there emerged a new political ideology, that of popular sovereignty. The Jeffersonian elitism was to be rejected in favor of direct rule by the people themselves (that is, the white citizens). Accordingly, the purpose of schools had to be changed again: Instead of serving as a selector of leaders, the schools were to serve as *equalizers*. Privilege and elitism were to be destroyed, and all men were to receive the same 'good common education'. In short, the school was to be the social institution to make all men equal.

Later in the 1800s and early 1900s, as the nation became increasingly more industrialized, there was a perceptible shift in Americans' attitude about the function schools were to be effecting. This was the 'land of opportunity', and the schools were expected to assure all persons equal opportunity for success in adulthood. Of course, it was assumed that the individual must be willing to work hard and have a high level of aspiration, but given these elements the school was seen to function as the sure stepladder to prosperity for him. Success literature and the mythology of HORATIO ALGER and ANDREW CARNEGIE abounded.

Some historians have chosen to impose explicit economic interpretations upon functional analyses of the evolution of the American educational system. GINTIS [1972], for example, has argued convincingly that the system of mass compulsory education assumed its present form primarily as the result of changing productive relations associated with the industrial revolution. Essentially, schools were perceived to perform the all-important function of supplying a properly socialized, stratified labor force. Indeed, the critical turning points in the history of American education coincided with the perceived failure of the educational system to fulfill this socializing role. At each of these critical periods many options were available as to which direction the schools should be turned, and these possibilities were openly discussed and debated. But the choices ultimately made were in correspondence to the new labor needs of an altered capitalistic system. For example, in the mid- to late nineteenth century the schools were transformed in accordance with the economy's need to generate a labor force compatible with the factory system from a predominantly agricultural populace. Somewhat later, the crisis in education corresponded to the economy's need to import peasant labor from Europe whose cultural inheritance and relationship to production were incompatible with an industrial wage-labor system. The eventual resolution of these crises was the formation of a hierarchical, centralized system of schools [GINTIS, 1972].

Related to this economic interpretation is what GREER [1972] has called 'The Great School Legend'. This asserts that the credit for building the American democracy should be given to the American public school system. According to the 'Legend', the public schools took the backward, poor, ill-prepared, illiterate immigrants – the 'huddled masses yearning to be free' – and educated them, americanized them, and molded them into the homogeneous, productive middle class that is now America's strength and pride. Unfortunately, the 'Legend' is just that – a legend. If it were true, as GREER [1972] has pointed out, the public schools today might work for the black urban poor, instead of merely insulting them with the erroneous and insidious comparison to the alleged success of the immigrant poor who, as claimed by the Legend, took such good advantage of public schools 50 years ago. The truth is that schools have always failed the American lower classes – white as well as nonwhite. In nearly every study of school effectiveness since the first one carried out in Chicago in 1898, more children have failed in urban public schools than have succeeded, both in absolute as well as relative numbers. Indeed, the upward mobility of the white lower class was never as speedy or as certain as conventional wisdom would insist. The 1920 census revealed that even the favored English and Welsh immigrants found at least half their group tied to the lowest, unskilled forms of labor; school dropout rates for all lower-class groups were in direct proportion to rates of adult employment; and the imposition of compulsory attendance at higher levels of education only served to push failure rates into the upper grades in large city schools during the 1920s and 30s. In short, during the period of industrialization and urbanization in America, the school served neither the function of equalizer nor of provider of equal opportunity, but rather it served as a sorter and reinforcer of the existing social order [GREER, 1972; PERKINSON, 1968].

One final historical note will be made here. It has become customary to view the use of standardized tests as a necessary consequence of industrial society. In fact, however, this consequence is more intimately connected with massive mobilization for modern war than it is to the fact of industrialization. It is well known that the pressures and exigencies of world war I laid the groundwork for the widespread utilization of intelligence tests in the military during the war and in schools after the war. It is not nearly as well known, however, that a similar set of conditions paved the way for the widespread acceptance of college-entrance qualifying examinations immediately after world war II [SCHUDSON, 1972]. At this time colleges were faced with overwhelming numbers of applicants – the normal age cohort plus military veterans returning to college – so for reasons of administrative efficiency and organization standardized examinations were nearly universally adopted in institutions of higher education. Furthermore, these institutions could convince themselves that they were justified in their actions, for the distinctions they were making among students were being accomplished by 'scientific' and 'objective' methods, thus preserving the democratic ideal.

To summarize, for 350 years Americans have looked to their schools to solve their social, political, and economic problems. The school system was the great panacea – albeit imperfect [PERKINSON, 1968]. Educational policy was determined by notions about the nature of human nature and about the desired form society was to take. The next section will discuss selected aspects of contemporary educational practice. Special attention will be given to the way in which prevailing conceptions of 'human nature' influence the form of educational practice, and, in turn, how educational practice influences the personal development of students.

Contemporary Educational Practice and Assumptions about Human Nature

Only two facets of contemporary educational practice will be dealt with here. These aspects – standardized testing and compensatory education – were selected because they are clear manifestations of the assumptions about human nature that underlie current formulations of educational policy.

Most American children have their first direct experience with the meritocratic structure of their society when they encounter standardized tests of achievement (or skill) early in elementary school. This experience will be repeated with increasing frequency thereafter as they move through the age-graded school structure, and quite likely even further testing will be encountered throughout their adult vocational life. For American youth, testing – with its consequent comparison against others – is a fact of life.

The interweaving of the notion of equality of opportunity into a meritocratic social order presumes that human beings are finite and comparable, that their usefulness and worth can be quantitatively measured, and that such measurement is a legitimate basis for grouping and stratifying. Accordingly, the omnipresence of tests in schools has engendered a set of concomitant attitudes and practices. Students learn early that education is a process of seeking out 'right' answers, and that those persons who can produce the most right answers are the best persons. Further, they learn that what is called the 'curriculum' is a series of courses, each of which is a set of activities directed toward that ultimate and final academic punctuation mark – the examination. And for those who have managed to maintain themselves near the top end of the test-score heap, there remains the prospect of taking a series of examinations to determine whether they are 'qualified' to experience four or more years of additional testing at the college level.[1] Of course, only those students are selected for colleges (via test scores) who will do well in colleges as they are now organized, thus putting a freeze on middle-class style and affording colleges an automatic legitimation and a rationale for nondevelopment. [See SCHUDSON, 1972, for an insightful discussion on the history of college-qualification examinations.] It does not seem inaccurate to say that for most youth, their educational experiences are more stratifying than satisfying.

This same belief that human experience – and thus human beings – can be quantified and compared is also fundamental to the current wave of compensatory education efforts. For these efforts this belief is translated into the implicit assumption that educational curricula and the social organization of schools are directed toward maintaining a single set of cultural attributes or standards. Perhaps this could be called the 'public culture'. This assumption provides the justification for the standardization of subject matter, codes of conduct, and classroom organization. The ethic of equal opportunity thus calls for intervention or compensatory programs to bring the so-called deprived or disadvantaged child up to 'normal'; in this way he can begin his competition with other children for educational and economic prizes from the same point in the starting gate.

Despite all the effort and resources that have been poured into compensatory programs, there is little indication that their professed goal has been achieved. Seen from a different light, the enduring support for ill-conceived and ineffective intervention programs may be an indication that despite society's equalitarian rhetoric, it persists in maintaining those conditions that restrain the disadvantaged from fully realizing their abilities. This view has been expressed well by FARBER and LEWIS [1972, p. 90]:

'... by focusing almost exclusively upon the educational deficits of the disadvantaged – by attending to a condition of impediment which presumably is a function of the life style of the impeded – those who embrace the compensatory strategy depoliticize the problem of unequal access to opportunity and thereby surround it with an aura of moral neutrality.'

[1] It was for these sorts of reasons that the Soviet Union declared in 1936 that psychometric examinations of schoolchildren were 'pseudoscientific' and creative of undesirable effects. The Russian rulers felt that these methods had permeated the Soviet educational system from the pedagogy of capitalist countries, where they are supposedly used to justify the class character of their educational systems [cf. BROŽEK, 1972].

It can thus be argued that society's persistence in pursuing the compensatory strategy, despite its lack of demonstrable success, is because these programs serve a *symbolic* function: A commitment is made to the attainment of equal access to opportunity by endorsing and funding special 'catch-up' programs for the disadvantaged and deprived. This symbolic attack on a social problem, therefore, serves the purpose of assuaging lingering doubts that we are not doing enough to help the poor and disadvantaged, but it also guards against asking those hard questions that might upset the status-quo interests. In short, the current conception of compensatory education is little more than 'progressive status-quoism' [FARBER and LEWIS, 1972]; it has the sound of farreaching change, but the fundamental problem itself remains untouched.

Testing and compensatory programs are but two aspects of the total complex of American educational practice. For the individual, the educational interlude of his early life serves to reinforce the notion that experience can be quantified, and that these quantities ultimately are used to identify, select, and appraise the 'best qualified' competitors for admission, advancement, and accolade within the meritocratic hierarchy.

The schools do well in inculcating and disseminating the 'Psychology of More' [LOOFT, 1971]. Children learn early that *much is good*, but *more* is better. As suggested earlier, the classroom is the environment where children are first introduced to this attitude, at least in a form that bears directly on their own lives. It is not long before one overhears young schoolchildren comparing their academic 'progress' – either against others (I got two more A's on my report card than you got) or against themselves (I got more A's this term than I got last term). The quantitative/more orientation inevitably leads toward a 'balance sheet' approach to personal identity, using the term of ERICH FROMM. The individual is directed toward quantifying his experience, and, therefore, he equates personal worth with countable things. Grades, income, possessions, lovers – all can be counted, compared, and competed for.

New Directions

Hopefully the previous discussion has made the point that the arguments put forth by scientists such as JENSEN [1969] and HERRNSTEIN [1971] are fully consistent with the educational, economic and social structures of the society in which these men teach and conduct research. A historical view of their work provides a valuable perspective for understanding the context of the present controversy stirred up by it. There have long been various sorts of appeals to justify the existing social order – the ability to speak the Greek language, Divine Order, 'survival-of-the-fittest' notions, and so on. Today there exists the danger that appeals to scientific authority may be used to legitimate class subordination. It probably would be unfair to label JENSEN and HERRNSTEIN as the latest apologists for social privilege (this has never been a very desirable topic for ethical defense), but the products of their industriousness – the 'hard data' of modern, scientific psychology – may nevertheless serve this purpose.

It was stated earlier in this paper that even the harshest critics of JENSEN and others have done little to diminish the significance of the ability/heredity argument. The critics, too, are enmeshed in the network of society – with all its attendant beliefs and unexamined assumptions. It would appear that the critics have only offered a *negation* to the JENSEN argument; that is, an antithesis has been put forth to counter the thesis. Unfortunately, to end the analysis only at negation leads to an implicit affirmation of the original thesis. The next – and most necessary – step is to move beyond both thesis and antithesis and work toward developing an acceptable synthesis. The remainder of this paper will present (perhaps with some degree of temerity) an analysis of this issue chiefly as it pertains to the educational system and its relationship with the larger social order. Perhaps some of these ideas will have value for the development of a new synthesis of understanding on this critical issue.

It first is crucial to emphasize that *expansion* has been a primary characteristic of the entire American system [MARX, 1970]. The history of this nation is one of unceasing accumulation of income, land, and population. The significance of the economic basis of this national orientation cannot be underestimated. As in all societies, formal education in America is the process of transposing an economic and social ideology into an individual, internalized, personalized matrix of values and self-reference system. With the omnipresent 'Psychology of More', individuals in this culture consume as they do – and hence acquire beliefs concerning consumption – because of the role consumption actively holds among the array of available alternatives for social expression. Accordingly, what might seem to be an irrational preoccupation with material goods and income is actually a quite logical response on the part of the individual in response to the central

orientation of the culture [GINTIS, 1972].[2] But in the process the context of
social activity is rendered less humane, for individuals are placed in competition with each other; the outcome is that both social and individual
welfare are diminished. Individual needs are transformed into desires for
goods and services; one's well-being is not found in what one *does* but in
what one *has*. In short, the economic institutions of capitalism invariably
sacrifice the healthy development of community, work, education, and
environment to the acquisition of capital and the expansion of marketable
goods and services. Community, work, education, and environment, therefore, become sources of frustration and disdain rather than desirable contexts for social relations. In a rather oblique fashion, GINTIS [1972] has
captured this idea most aptly: 'The "sales pitch" of Madison Avenue is
accepted because, in the given context, it is true. It may not be much, but
it's all we got' [p. 82].

All of these institutions and processes are maintained, as has been argued
here, by a particular set of assumptions, by a particular model of man –
that the human being is consumptive, reactive, and is imbued with the
'Psychology of More'. Indeed, most of the contemporary radical critics of
the educational system insist that what goes on in schools (and, therefore,
society) does not reflect the true nature of man at all. Their rallying cry is
'Schools are dehumanizing and repressive'. Their proposals range from re-
forming present schools into 'free' or 'open' schools to doing away with
schools altogether. It would seem, though, that these arguments presuppose
the existence of a parasocial human 'essence', or a fundamental quality of
human existence that is outside the realm of social derivation or influence.
Thus, 'Man is essentially good' or 'Man is essentially evil', and so forth.
But this view, it would seem, only offers another kind of absolute human
standard, one that inheres within the individual and that is unassociated

---

[2] This is the essence of the brilliant analysis by CHOMSKY [1972] of HERRNSTEIN's
[1971] position. CHOMSKY has argued that HERRNSTEIN's notion of an evolving hereditary
meritocracy (in which transmittable wealth and power accrue to those with high mental
ability) is fundamentally a very materialistic interpretation. HERRNSTEIN's proposal is rife
with the 'Psychology of More': People labor only for material gain, for psychological
rewards are not sufficient. CHOMSKY has cleverly proposed an alternative interpretation
of this notion of an IQ-determined meritocracy:
'One might speculate, rather plausibly, that wealth and power tend to accrue to those
who are ruthless, cunning, avaricious, self-seeking, lacking in sympathy and compassion,
subservient to authority, willing to abandon principle for material gain, and so on.
Furthermore, these less endearing traits might well be as heritable as IQ, and might out-
weigh IQ as factors in gaining material reward' [CHOMSKY, 1972, p. 28].

with the social experience it generates. To arrive at the synthesis called for here, it perhaps is most desirable to reject the notion of intrinsic human 'essences' altogether and adopt the assumption that all persons are uniquely developed by their actions as articulated through social life. Most individual activity is not solely personal, but rather it is founded in contexts of social interaction, structured by the legitimate and approved roles available to the individual in his work, community, or educational environments. It follows, then, that the character of individual participation in these domains – the defining roles one assumes as a worker, community member, or student – is a fundamental determinant of personal well-being and development.

If this tenet – that 'human nature' is created through one's own actions in social contexts – is accepted, then it is essential that any proposal for societal change must begin with the recognition that people are now alienated from their most vital defining characteristic – their productive activity. Individuals must be allowed to exercise direct control over the structuring of their various social environments. Power must be allocated in a way that insures that the workings of society are matched to the needs and aspirations of its participating members; the quality of their participation – in whatever form it may take – must be such that there is the promotion of full development of self-understanding and social effectiveness.

A primary thesis of this paper is that schooling practices have been greatly responsible for creating and maintaining the belief system that is reflected in all aspects of society and of which the JENSEN controversy is only one manifestation. It is clear that if change is desired, the schools themselves will have to undergo radical transformations. Teachers must become genuine allies of the students and citizens they serve. Their pedagogical activities cannot remain a technical function, a benign favor bestowed from above and afar. Schools and teachers must become actively involved in the political process of changing the rules now ordering the allocation of cultural and economic benefits. The actions to be taken, of course, will carry certain attendant attitudes.

The following assumptions are essential to the view being promoted here: (a) Educational endeavors must be freed from the mindless conformity to the dictates of the 'public culture'. (b) Personal worth and dignity can assume a great diversity of forms; these qualities cannot be totally defined by a single standard as represented by a test of intelligence or achievement. (c) It must not be insisted that all children must be educated to all facets of the 'public culture' (with the consequent threat that if they do not learn accordingly, they will assuredly become stigmatized personal failures and burdens upon society). (d) There must be a willingness to exchange some of the ever-present concern for organizational efficiency in educational system (and society in general) for a pluralistic attitude that values and encourages the development of a multiplicity of life styles and abilities.

It seems certain that the poor and the alienated will not long continue to accept the stigma of failure that is created by the application of compensatory-education and standardized-testing strategies. The growing militancy on the part of the nonwhite poor in relation to traditional educational panaceas and strategies is only one indication of what the future has in store. The longer the educational system is allowed to be guided by these inadequate, constraining attitudes, the more militant the resistance will become, and the more estranged educators will become from those they presume to help. The necessary political goal that must be worked toward at this time is the nurturance of persons who demand control over their lives and respectable outlets for their productive activities and who are conscious of the true nature of their relationship to their society. With the evolution of a society composed of these kinds of individuals, the JENSEN controvery will someday be rendered irrelevant and viewed only as a historical – although unfortunate – curiosity.

References

BROŽEK, J.: To test or not to test: trends in the Soviet Union. J. Hist. Beh. Sci. 8: 243–248 (1972).

CHOMSKY, N.: IQ tests. Building blocks for the new class system. Ramparts 11 (1): 24–30 (1972).

FARBER, B. and LEWIS, M.: Compensatory education and social justice. Peabody J. Educ. 23: 85–96 (1972).

GINTIS, H.: Toward a political economy of education. A radical critique of Ivan Illich's Deschooling Society. Harvard Educ. Rev. 42: 70–96 (1972).

GREER, C.: The great school legend (Basic Books, New York 1972).

HERRNSTEIN, R.: IQ. Atlantic 228: 43–64 (Sept. 1971).

JENSEN, A.R.: How much can we boost IQ and scholastic achievement? Harvard Educ. Rev. 39: 1–123 (1969).

LOOFT, W.R.: The psychology of more. Amer. Psychol. 26: 561–565 (1971).

MARX, L.: American institutions and ecological ideals. Science 170: 945–952 (1970).

PERKINSON, H.J.: The imperfect panacea. American faith in education, 1865–1965 (Random House, New York 1968).

SCHUDSON, M.S.: Organizing the 'meritocracy'. A history of the College Entrance Examination Board. Harvard Educ. Rev. 42: 34–69 (1972).

Request reprints from: Dr. W.R. LOOFT, College of Human Development, Pennsylvania State University, *University Park, PA 16802* (USA)

Human Develop. *16:* 33–52 (1973)

Alternative Conceptions of Intellectual Functioning[1]

S. R. TULKIN and M. J. KONNER

State University of New York at Buffalo, Buffalo, N.Y., and
Harvard University, Cambridge, Mass.

Abstract. Research which discusses group differences in intellectual functioning utilizes a very limited definition of intelligence. Intelligence is not assessed within cultural context, and little regard is paid to intellectual activities which do not involve the manipulation of abstract concepts. This orientation de-emphasizes the potential development of other human capacities which might be even more helpful in adapting to or advancing our civilization by emphasizing child-rearing patterns aimed primarily at the development of abstract thought.

Key Words
Cross-cultural
Intellectual functioning
Cultural relativism
Abstract thinking
Nonintellectual capacities
Child rearing

Most researchers who discuss group differences in intellectual functioning have adopted a definition of intelligence which is considerably more limited than the typical dictionary definition in which intelligence is described as the 'capacity for understanding and for other forms of adaptive behavior' [American College Dictionary, 1959]. Researchers have defined a set of arbitrary tasks – most of which involve the manipulation of abstract concepts – and have assessed the abilities of people from widely different experiential backgrounds to complete these tasks. This approach to developmental psychology is consistent with the 'capitalistic' orientation of Anglo-American countries, in which all individuals are evaluated against single standards, and are seen as being in competition against each other [Riegel, 1972]. This orientation limits our understanding of intellectual development in several ways.

[1] We would like to thank the Department of Psychology of the State University of New York at Buffalo, especially Dr. MURRAY LEVINE, for providing the opportunity for us to meet and collaborate on the present paper.

First, little attention has been paid to the relation between the 'experimental tasks' and the skills needed for 'adaptive behavior' in one's own culture or reference group. COLE *et al.* [1971], for example, found that American adults performed more poorly than nonliterate Kpelle (Liberian) farmers on a task involving the sorting of leaves into categories based on whether the leaves were from vines or trees. This says nothing about Americans' 'capacity for understanding and for other forms of adaptive behavior'. Similarly, FJELLMAN [1971] compared schooled and unschooled Akamba (Kenyan) adolescents and found that when classifying geometric shapes the schooled subjects used more abstract, and the unschooled more concrete, principles of classification. This, of course, supports previous research [BRUNER *et al.*, 1966] demonstrating that schooling is related to the development of abstract thinking skills. However, FJELLMAN [1971] also had subjects classify animals – a task which is more closely tied to 'adaptive behavior' in Akamba life. On this task, she found that the unschooled children used more abstract (e.g. domestic vs. wild) and the schooled more concrete (e.g. color) classifying principles. Thus their respective positions in a developmental sequence are reversed depending not even on the nature of the task but merely on the objects to be operated upon. The failure of many researchers to examine the 'cultural relevance' of their experimental tasks has led to questionable statements of fundamental differences in thinking among different populations. This argument is pursued in more detail below.

A second, more basic, question is whether the Western world's emphasis on the mastery of abstract conceptual skills has blinded us to the potential development of other capacities which might be even more helpful in 'adapting' or in 'advancing' our civilization. Maybe, in fact, the groups that are 'deficient' on various arbitrary 'intellectual' tasks devised by psychologists, are in fact deficient only in relation to these tasks, or to certain classes of objects, or to objects in general, or to the printed word. These same groups may prove to be superior in handling conceptual problems of a psychological, social or even sociological nature, and this ability may prove to be more crucial by far for continued human adaptation and survival.

In the section below, we present some alternative perspectives on Western man's (or more precisely, the Western psychologist's) definition of intelligence. In the following section we will describe instances in which researchers in the United States have failed to recognize possible alternative explanations for the results they have reported, and thus contributed to the development of biases which continue to have an impact on psychology.

Varieties of Intelligence

Inductive Processes of Conceptualization

Substantial evidence has recently emerged which demonstrates the exist-ence of sophisticated knowledge in several fields of science among primitive cultures. The time-honored notion that 'primitive man' lives in a state of total ignorance completely hedged by superstition, is simply no longer tenable. LEVI-STRAUSS [1966] has summarized the evidence for an encyclo-pedic knowledge about plants in many 'primitive' societies. Interestingly, he points out that this knowledge had to be discovered by botanists. The anthropologists and missionaries who had reported on nonliterate botanical science simply did not know enough botany to assess what their subjects knew. Similarly, in a recent study among the Kalahari Desert Bushmen [BLURTON JONES and KONNER, 1972], several ideas about nonliterate science were formulated. In terms of industrial technology and other Western con-cepts of progress, the Kalahari Bushmen are the most 'backward' to be found anywhere in the world today. Yet the range and exactness of their knowledge of animal behavior, including some of the most recent findings of scientists in Africa, is substantial. What struck the investigators most emphatically was the *method* of obtaining and assessing this knowledge. This method was unmistakeably similar to what we know as science.

A series of seminars was conducted to gather information about the thinking of the Bushmen regarding animal behavior. They were attended by BLURTON JONES (an ethologist), KONNER (an anthropologist), and from four to seven Bushmen experienced and knowledgeable in hunting. As scientific discussions the seminars were among the most stimulating the Western observers had ever attended. Questions were raised and tentative answers *(hypotheses)* were advanced. Hypotheses were always labeled as to the degree of certainty with which the speaker adhered to them, which was related to the type of data on which the hypothesis was based. For example, the Bushmen differentiated among the following types of evidence: (1) I saw it with my eyes; (2) I didn't see it with my eyes but I saw the tracks. Here is how I inferred it from the tracks; (3) I didn't see it with my own eyes or see the tracks but I heard it from many people who saw it (or a few people who saw it, or one person who saw it); (4) It's not certain because I didn't see it with my eyes, or talk directly with people who saw it. The men frequently challenged each other's views, and discussions proceded to more or less certain conclusions. To summarize: the natural world was observed;

hypotheses about its details and relations among them were advanced, these were allocated to different levels of certainty depending on how they were induced; the induction procedure was specified; competing hypotheses were advanced and belief allocated between them in accord with the same rules; some conclusion was reached, even if just an agreement that the problem had yet to be solved; such conclusions were remembered and communicated to others. In other words, the resulting body of knowledge was detailed, wide-ranging, and accurate.

In retrospect, it is not so surprising. Human survival has depended upon this kind of knowledge for five million years. One would expect people to have arrived at a good method of getting it, and scientific induction and hypothesis-testing is, of course, a good method. What is surprising is that some observers believe such faculties of mental process to be the domain of industrial man alone. Do they imagine that a few centuries of physics and chemistry have abruptly transformed the human brain so as to make it capable of science? All that we know about evolution makes this notion unacceptable. Indeed there would have had to be some characteristic of man's environment of evolutionary adaptedness, the hunting and gathering way of life, which would cause a brain with these inductive and analytic capacities to evolve. The above-described acquisition of knowledge about animals, which is not restricted to the Bushmen (LAUGHLIN [1968] describes similarly sophisticated knowledge among the Eskimo) certainly contributed to this selection pressure. But one can see that the need to improve the process of hunting itself was also important. The process of tracking, specifically, involves patterns of inference, hypothesis-testing and discovery that tax the best inferential and analytic capacities of the human mind. Determining, from tracks, the movements of animals, their timing, whether they are wounded and if so how, and predicting how far they will go and in which direction and how fast, all involve repeated activation of hypotheses, trying them out against new data, integrating them with previously known facts about animal movements, rejecting the ones that do not stand up, and finally getting a reasonable fit, which adds up to meat in the pot.

Man is the only hunting mammal with a poorly developed sense of smell. He could only have come to hunting through intellectual evolution. If this argument is valid, the notion that different human groups could have different inductive capacities would be inherently illogical, since all groups have shared the same five million years of hunting, and whatever has happened since plays a relatively insignificant role in terms of time – and time is what is needed for brain evolution to take place.

Noninduction Processes of Conceptualization

There are also several categories of noninductive thinking which have been institutionalized in nonliterate, or at least non-Western, cultures just as inductive inference and syllogistic deduction have in Western science. Although these types of thinking are often ignored by psychologists, or thought of as 'primitive' mental processes, it can be argued that they also represent advanced forms of mental functioning.

Animistic thought. MARGARET MEAD [1932], in a classic paper describing what was surely one of the first Piaget-based cross-cultural studies, discusses an experiment conducted among the Manus people of the Admiralty Islands. The experiment was designed to test the notion of PIAGET, LEVY-BRUHL, WERNER, and others that 'primitive' systems of thought, in this case *animism,* were similar to the thought of children, and that animism is a primary stage in the development of reality-based thinking. MEAD [1932] found that animistic thought occupied a large part in the mental life of Manus adults. This included a belief in ghosts ('ghosts occupy fully a third of adult thought and conversation'), a belief in supernatural animals which cause illness, and the imputing of intent to inanimate objects. MEAD [1932] also observed and tested 41 children in various standard situations, collected 32,000 drawings, and administered an inkblot interpretation test. The children ranged in age from 3 to prepubertal.

The results were consistent in demonstrating that the animistic ideas which figure so prominently in the thought of Manus adults play no part whatsoever in the thought of Manus children. Children virtually never produced the animistic explanations of natural phenomena codified by the culture. In fact they often ridiculed them. The experiment demonstrates that animistic thinking is not the only type of thinking which primitive people are capable of; in fact these thought patterns must be acquired in the course of growing up. More generally, adult nonliterate animism cannot be considered a holdover from childhood thought patterns, but on the contrary must be considered and investigated as an independent system of advanced abstract thought. The elaborate nature of adult Manus animistic thought is itself worthy of study [MEAD, 1932].

Kinship systems. For some decades the main subject matter of social anthropology has been kinship, or nonliterate systems of classifying people in accordance with established rules of blood and marriage relation [LEVI-STRAUSS, 1969]. Functions of kinship systems include smoothly distributing women over a field of potential husbands, governance of corporate land tenure, economic distribution through systemitized gift-giving, inheritance of wealth, status and responsibility, and allocation of children to caretakers.

Kinship considerations occupy a much more prominent place in the thought of 'primitive' people than in our own, because for us these functions are discharged by a decision-making hierarchy. Kinship systems are variable in the exact nature of their specifications and also in the degree of their complexity. The most complex, such as the multi-section marriage-class systems of Australia, have long caused enthnographers to throw up their hands in despair after many efforts at understanding [ELKIN, 1964]. Even relatively simple ones, like that of the Zhun/twa Bushmen, may provide evidence of complex thought processes.

Studies based on cognitive tests [BRUNER *et al.,* 1966] have called into question the ability of nonliterate peoples to reclassify a set of objects in more than one way, an ability reflecting one of the higher stages of PIAGET's concrete operations. Other studies have argued that this finding is partially explained by the unfamiliarity of the material to be classified [COLE *et al.,* 1971]. One need not even administer tests, however; the very basis of the Bushmen and other kinship systems lies precisely in its classification of the same human 'objects' in two separate ways according to very distinct principles. The first is an ordinary reckoning of kinship through blood and marriage, with a classification of individuals according to degrees of these relations. The second is a fictive system based on the *name* relation. This gives a person a special relationship to a child who takes his name. This child then addresses his namesake's relatives as if they were related to him in the same way they are to his namesake. Since his namesake is usually related to him in the first place, this results in his addressing and conceptualizing each of the people in his social world as having two relations to him. Thus, his great-aunt may be his mother, with both relations having significance.

It would be of obvious interest to examine the acquisition of this dual classification system in the growing child, but this is only one of many studies which might be done concerning the cognitive structure of kinship systems and how they are developed and learned.

Totemism and myth. Subsequent to his studies of kinship, LEVI-STRAUSS [1963, 1966] turned his attention to other aspects of primitive thought, specifically to totemism and myth. In the course of this work he has developed a number of theories about how 'primitive' thought functions, and made an effort to show that much of Western thought works, or could work, the same way. He presented a new solution to the anthropological problem of totemism by suggesting that totems themselves do not directly represent the human groups using their names, but instead, the *relationship* among these groups is symbolized by the relationship among the totems. This type of system utilized the thought process, familiar from intelligence test problems, 'A is to B as C is to...?'. Later LEVI-STRAUSS [1966] extended this principle to many other aspects of 'primitive' thought, especially in the area of myth. He appears to have unearthed a great complexity of thought processes somewhat foreign to our own, and begun the task of describing them.

It would seem appropriate for cognitive and developmental psychologists to turn part of their attention to his work, to try to understand 'savage' thought in psychological terms, and to begin the serious study of how such thought develops in the child. Such research would replace the glib psychological presumption that 'savage' thought is at a lower stage of development with a real understanding of how these complex mental systems grow out of their own lower stages, perhaps in a kind of sequence very different from our own.

Zen. Some non-Western systems of thought involve methods for de-activating 'normal' thought processes. One of these is Zen [WATTS, 1957]. In this view, the goal of understanding is achieved through a kind of perception which is held to be incompatible with hypothetico-deductive thinking. It is a perception achieved through *not* thinking. The latter is not a simple task related to laziness but is on the contrary the result of a complex mental discipline. Like the most advanced forms of deductive and inductive thought, it requires extreme concentration and the shutdown of most normal mental process (which is largely associative) to avoid distraction. Thought processes are relaxed to produce heightened perception (and the knowledge that results from heightened perception). MACCOBY and MODIANO [1966] noted that people socialized into the modern industrialized world often lose the ability to experience. 'They are', the authors suggested, 'like people who see a painting immediately in terms of its style, period, and influences but with no sense of its uniqueness'. In view of these other routes to knowledge, the imbalance in our educational system in favor of scientific and other analytic thought processes may be questioned.

The feeling side of man. A specialized use of associative thinking which is important to certain processes in art but which also has many applications outside art is thinking about feelings. Progress in the understanding of feelings is impeded by efforts to think about them strictly 'scientifically', that is, using modes of thought designed to function best in the absence of feelings.

In the recent resurgence of American black culture, with its attendant anti-white feeling, the point has been repeatedly stressed that some blacks find whites to be inferior in their ability to think about and acquire knowledge about feelings and, in a related way, about people. This point is summarized in the concepts of 'soul' and 'hip' [CLEAVER, 1968; MAILER, 1959]. JAMES BALDWIN wrote in *The fire next time* [quoted by CLEAVER, 1968]: 'White people cannot, in the generality, be taken as models of how to live. Rather, the white man is himself in sore need of new standards, which will release him from his confusion and place him once again in fruitful communion with the depths of his own being' (p. 65).

What is needed is to get knowledge about one's self, about one's deepest feelings, about how to live. The black psychiatrist FRANZ FANON [1968] has written: 'All European thought has unfolded in places which were increasingly more deserted and more encircled by precipices; and thus it was that the custom grew up in those places of very seldom meeting man. A permanent dialogue with oneself and an increasingly obscene narcissism never ceased to prepare the way for a half delirious state, where intellectual work became suffering and the reality was not at all that of a living man, working and creating himself, but rather words, different combinations of words, and the tensions springing from the meanings contained in words' (p. 313). This view, again, finds Western thought wanting in its ability to deal with human beings and human problems: 'The custom grew up in those places of very seldom meeting man.'

/Third World spokesmen in general view Western thought as appallingly excellent when applied to problems of strictly 'intellectual' concern, but totally and absurdly helpless when applied to human concerns or feelings. One example is an interesting experiment recently reported by MADSEN [1971], who found a higher level of cooperation among Mexican than among Anglo-American children. MADSEN [1971] also reported an increase in maladaptive competition with age among the Anglo-American. Other researchers [MACCOBY and MODIANO, 1966] have noted that our socialization patterns may be producing children who exchange 'a spontaneous, less alienated relationship to the world for a more sophisticated outlook which concentrates on using, exchanging, or cataloguing... (They have warned that) what industrialized man gains in an increased ability to formulate, to reason, and to code the ever more numerous bits of complex information he acquires, he may lose in decreased sensitivity to people and events' (p. 269).

A final piece of testimony comes from KENNETH KAUNDA [1966], the President of Zambia. He has remarked that the thing that most surprised and shocked him on his first visit to Europe was the existence of old age homes. He wrote that when the first old age home appears in Zambia, Zambians will know that their goal – achieving progress while retaining their humanity – has failed. We rarely think about old age homes, while an African leader finds them evidence of the most basic human and *intellectual* failure. We do not think about them, probably because they are too hard to think about, because we have not been trained to focus the resources of our intellects on problems which call into play so many deep feelings. It is in such matters that Western thought has a great deal to learn from studying non-Western thought systems, which have long specialized in thinking about human beings and in thinking about feelings. Such study has barely begun.

Effects of Ethnocentrism on Research[2]

Psychology's reliance on the norms of the white middle-class as standards against which to measure other groups has produced a biased picture of the strengths and weaknesses of various subgroups in the United States. This philosophy also impeded the advancement of developmental psychology by encouraging studies which simply compare different groups on various dependent variables with meager, if any, attempts to understand the *processes* by which these skills develop.

Need for Cultural Relativism

One issue of current interest to psychologists is whether black ghetto residents are less able to communicate verbally, or are simply less proficient in 'Standard English'. Some studies have shown that lower-class subjects are verbally deficient, and the deficits are 'not entirely attributable to implicit "middle-class" orientations' [KRAUSS and ROTTER, 1968]. Other experts argue that Black English is a fully-formed linguistic system in its own right, with its own grammatical rules and unique history [BARATZ and SHUY, 1969; DILLARD, 1972; LABOV, 1967; STEWART, 1967, 1969a]. These critics state that black language is 'different from standard American English, but no less complex, communicative, rich, or sophisticated' [SROUFE, 1970]; and argue that research reporting language 'deficits' among black children reflects only the middle-class orientation of the research instruments and procedures. Supporting this argument, BIRREN and HESS [1968] concluded that, studies of peer groups in spontaneous interaction in Northern ghetto areas shown that there is rich verbal culture in constant use.

---

[2] This discussion is taken largely from S.R. TULKIN, An analysis of the concept of cultural deprivation. Develop. Psychol. *6:* 326–339 (1972).

Negro children in the vernacular culture cannot be considered "verbally deprived" if one observes them in a favorable environment – on the contrary, their daily life is a pattern of continual verbal stimulation, contest, and imitation' (p. 137).

Similarly, CHANDLER and ERICKSON [1968] observed *naturally occurring* group interaction and reported data which argues against the findings of BERNSTEIN [1960, 1961] and others that middle-class children more commonly use 'elaborated' linguistic codes while lower classes typically speak with 'restricted' codes. CHANDLER and ERICKSON [1968] found that the use of 'restricted' or 'elaborated' linguistic codes was not as closely related to the social class of speakers as had been suggested by other researchers. 'Both inner city and suburban groups... were found to shift back and forth between use of relatively "restricted" linguistic codes and relatively "elaborated" codes. These shifts were closely related to apparent changes in the degree of shared context between group members... Examples of extremely abstract and sophisticated inquiry among inner city Negro young people were found in which a highly "restricted" linguistic code was employed. The use of "concrete" terms by Negro young people does not appear to necessarily limit inquiry, since the concrete terms are often employed in describing examples of actual behavior which are selected to illustrate an unstated "abstract" proposition' (p. 2).

If Black English and Standard English are simply different languages, one cannot be seen as more deficient than the other [SROUFE, 1970]. Most schools, however, demand that students use Standard English, and frequently black children who have been classified by their schools as 'slow learners' are able to read passages of Black English with amazing speed and accuracy [STEWART, 1969b]. Similarly, FOSTER [1969] found that the introduction of nonstandard English dialect increased the ability of 10th grade disadvantaged students 'to comprehend, to recall, and to be fluent and flexible in providing titles for verbal materials'. Black students also scored higher than white students on FOSTER's [1970] Jive Analogy Test[3]. WILLIAMS and RIVERS [1972] have also reported that black children who were administered a 'dialect-fair version' of Basic Concepts scored significantly higher than a control group of children who were administered the standard version.

This argument does not imply that the teaching of Standard English is an infringement of the rights of minority cultures. It is necessary that students learn Standard English, but there is a difference between emphasizing

---

[3] H.L. FOSTER, personal communication to S.R. TULKIN (1971).

the development of positive skills which may facilitate a successful adaptation to a particular majority culture, versus devaluing a group of people who may not emphasize the development of these particular skills. As BARATZ and BARATZ [1970] suggested, research should be undertaken to discover the different but not pathological forms of minority group behavior. 'Then and only then can programs be created that utilize the child's differences as a means of helping him acculturate to the mainstream while maintaining his individual identity and cultural heritage' (p. 47).

Parent-child interaction. Another example of the lack of cultural relativity is found in studies of parent-child interaction. The guiding philosophy of many researchers seems to be that (a) optimal development consists of the skills possessed by middle-class children in the United States; and therefore, (b) all mothers should interact with their infants in the style of US middle-class mothers. Both of these assumptions are questionable.

It is interesting that social scientists are reasonably tolerant of child-rearing practices observed in other cultures which would be devalued if reported in a minority group in the United States. REBELSKY and ABELES [1969], for example, observed American and Dutch mothers with their 0-3-month-old infants. They found that a Dutch baby typically slept in a low closed bed with a canopy overhead. Dutch mothers kept the infant's room cool – 'for health reasons' – necessitating infants being 'tightly covered under blankets, often tied into the crib with strings from their sheets'. Further, the authors reported comparisons showing that 'American mothers looked at, held, fed, talked to, smiled at, patted, and showed more affection to their babies more often than did Dutch mothers'. These findings, however, were not used to condemn Dutch mothers. The authors related the differences in parental behavior to cultural variations in the parents' conceptions of infancy. For example, they noted that: 'Even if a (Dutch) parent sees a child awake and wanting to play or look around, ...he is not likely to respond to this wish or to the behavior which implies this wish because of fear of "spoiling" the baby (stated by 9 of the 11 mothers in Holland), or because of the belief that a baby in this age range should sleep and not play or stay awake' (1969, pp. 16–17).

Observations also revealed that Dutch infants had fewer toys with which to play. By three months of age, almost half of the Dutch babies still had no toys within sight or touch. The authors explained that Dutch mothers were concerned that 'toys might keep the babies awake, or overstimulate them'. There were also cultural differences in the mothers' reactions to their infants crying. 'Crying meant a call for help to US mothers; they often reported lactating when they heard the cry. In Holland, crying was considered a part of a baby's behavior, good for the lungs and not always something to stop. In addition, though a mother might hear the cry in Holland and interpret it as a hunger cry, she still would not respond if it was not time for the scheduled feeding' (1969, pp. 7–8).

REBELSKY and ABELES [1969] did not suggest that Dutch mothers were rejecting or depriving their infants. They did not argue that intervention was necessary to change the patterns of mother-infant interaction. They concluded, instead, that both US and Dutch cultures 'may be training very different kinds of people, yet with each culture wanting the ones they produce'. Such data reported for a group of lower-income American mothers might be followed by a call for a massive intervention program, or possibly the removal of the infants from their homes.

A similar cultural comparison was reported by CAUDILL and WEINSTEIN [1966, 1969] who investigated maternal behavior in Japan and the United States. The authors reported that American mothers talked more to their infants, while Japanese mothers more frequently lulled and rocked their infants. These differences were seen as reflecting different styles of mothering. 'The style of the American mother seems to be in the direction of stimulating her baby to respond... whereas the style of the Japanese mother seems to be more in the direction of soothing and quieting her baby' (1966, p. 18).

In both cultures, the 'style' of mothering was influenced by the prevailing conception of infancy. CAUDILL and WEINSTEIN [1969] reported that in Japan 'the infant is seen more as a separate biological organism who from the beginning, in order to develop, needs to be drawn into increasingly interdependent relations with others. In America, the infant is seen more as a dependent biological organism who, in order to develop, needs to be made increasingly independent of others' (p. 15).

American mothers, following their conception of infancy, pushed their infants to respond and to be active; Japanese mothers, also following their conception of infancy, attempted to foster reduced independent activity and greater reliance on others. As a part of this pattern, the Japanese tended to place less emphasis on clear verbal communication. CAUDILL and WEINSTEIN [1969] reasoned that 'such communication implies self-assertion and the separate identity and independence of the person' which would be contrary to the personality which Japanese mothers were attempting to build into their children. Thus, in Japan, as in Holland, mothers related to their infants in a manner consistent with their beliefs and values.

CAUDILL and WEINSTEIN [1969] also reported data showing that according to American 'standards', the Japanese infants might be considered 'deficient'. They engaged in less positive vocalization and spent less time with toys and other objects: 'The Japanese infant', they said, 'seems passive – he spends much more time simply lying awake in his crib or on a zabuton (a flat cushion) on the floor.' The authors further reported that a study by ARAI et al. [1958] found that – compared to American norms – Japanese infants showed a steady decline on tests of language and motor development from 4 to 36 months of age. CAUDILL and WEINSTEIN [1969], however, remained relativistic. They commented that although ARAI et al. [1958] seemed somewhat distressed that the 'Japanese mothers were so bound up in the lives of their infants that they interfered with the development of their infants in ways which made it difficult to meet the American norms', they did not share the Japanese authors' concern: 'We do not believe that the differences we find are necessarily indications of a better or a worse approach to human life, but rather that such differences are a part of an individual's adjustment to his culture.' Again, it is doubtful if the same conclusion would have been reached were the data collected from a minority subculture in the United States.

Another report of mother-infant interaction [KONNER, in press] notes that children of the Kalahari Bushmen receive much more physical contact from their mothers than do American infants. Compared to the Bushmen, the American infants could be considered to be 'deprived' of physical stimulation. KONNER notes, however, that the infants' experiences in each culture are related to the nature of the culture: The Bushmen infant is growing up in a world where survival arises from mutual economic dependence, whereas the world of the American infants favors competition and independent mobility.

Jewish subcultures. A final example of the need for cultural relativism involves a study of Ashkenazic and Sephardic Jews in Brooklyn [GROSS, 1967]. Both groups were solidly middle class, and lived only two blocks apart. Both had been long-established in this country and spoke English in their homes. On entering school, however, the Sephardic children averaged 17 points lower on a standard IQ test, a 'deficit' similar to that often reported for black Americans.

The author pointed out that it is generally assumed that inferior performance in school necessarily reflects deprivation and lack of opportunity. He argued, on the contrary, that each culture has its own ideas of what is important – some emphasize one skill, some another. Despite their children's lower IQ scores the Sephardic mothers were not deprived, however one defines the term: In many cases they had maids, and country homes. The Sephardic mothers were all native born, high school graduates, and none worked. The children were raised with privilege, money and comfort, but their level of academic readiness was similar to that of their underprivileged Israeli counterparts.

GROSS [1967] explained that the difference was related to cultural tradition: The two communities represented different routes into the middle class – the Ashkenazim through success in school and the Sephardim through success in the marketplace. The author concluded that educational unpreparedness could be found among the 'financially well-to-do' as well as among the lower classes, and suggested that this finding should be a 'caution signal to social engineers'. GROSS [1967] questioned those who advocate changing lower-class Negro life to conform to the life styles and values of middle-class whites, and suggested that there was an element of 'white colonialism' in the attempt to 'reshape the economically underprivileged in the image of the education-minded intellectually oriented academicians'.

GROSS' [1967] final point merits expansion, because intervention is a big business in the United States today. The federal government is spending large amounts of money on intervention programs, and some social scientists fear that the interventionists will totally disregard subcultural systems in their attempts to 'save' the 'deprived' children. 'When we force people of another culture to make an adjustment to ours, by that much we are destroying the integrity of their personalities. When too many adjustments of this sort are required too fast, the personality disintegrates and the result is an alienated, dissociated individual who cannot feel really at home in either culture' [LEHMER, 1969, p. 4].

Politics and Cultural Differences

Finally, social scientists need to consider the way in which the majority culture, by its tolerance for social, political, and economic inequality, actually contributes to the development, in some subgroups, of the very characteristics which it considers 'deprived' [RYAN, 1971]. Responsibility, then, lies not with the subpopulations – for being 'deprived' – but rather with the 'total environmental structure that disenfranchises, alienates (and) disaffects' [HILLSON, 1970]. FANTINI [1969] echoed this argument when he suggested that the 'problem' of disadvantaged school children may not be rooted in the learner's 'environmental and cultural deficiencies' but rather with the system – 'the school and its educational process'. He suggested the need for reorientation 'from our present "student-fault" to a stronger "system-fault" position'.

One of the most obvious 'system-faults' – and one that is quite relevant to intellectual development – is inadequate medical care for the poor. Social scientists investigating 'cultural deprivation' have paid insufficient attention to the ways in which poor *physical health,* both of mothers during pregnancy and of infants early in life, can influence the child's developmental progress. The incidences of inadequate prenatal nutrition, premature births, and complications of delivery which can lead to brain injuries, are all greater among lower-income and nonwhite groups [ABRAMOWICZ and KASS, 1966; KNOBLOCK and PASAMANICK, 1962]. The effects of these medical differences are not unknown. KAGAN [1965] noted that one of the possible consequences of minimal brain damage during the perinatal and early postnatal periods is 'increased restlessness and distractability, and inabiliy to inhibit inappropriate responses during the preschool and early school years'. BROCKMAN and RICCIUTI [1971] also documented the effects of malnutrition on developing cognitive skills. We do not know the extent to which developmental 'deficits' of lower-income and minority group children can be traced to these differences in their *medical* histories. This is a clear-cut case where responsibility for deprivation falls mainly on the *majority* culture.

Delay of gratification and future orientation. Society as a whole is responsible for other behavior patterns observed in 'deprived' groups. LIEBOW [1967] argued that many of the behavior patterns he observed among lower-class blacks were 'a direct response to the conditions of lower class Negro life...'. His most cogent example involved the 'delay of gratification' variable. The frequent finding that lower-class (usually black) children prefer a smaller reward given immediately rather than a larger reward given later is often cited as a serious handicap to their schoolwork. It is often hypothesized that the child-rearing practices employed by lower-class parents lead children to prefer immediate gratification; and attempts are being made to change these practices and to teach the children to defer gratification. LIEBOW's analysis astutely demonstrates that, although socialization patterns may encourage behaviors which are seen as reflecting a preference for immediate gratification, the socialization patterns do not represent the primary determinant of this pattern. LIEBOW [1967] argued that the so-called preference for immediate gratification derives from the conditions of life encountered in this population. The *realities of life* represent the causal agent; the child-rearing patterns are only intermediary variables. The importance of LIEBOW's argument merits thorough examination. 'What appears as a "present time" orientation to the outside observer is, to the man experiencing it, as much a future orientation as that of his middle class counterpart. The difference between the two men lies not so much in their different orientations to time as in their different orientations to future time or more specifically, to their different futures. ...As for the future, the young streetcorner man has a fairly good picture of it... It is a future in which every-

GOSHEN COLLEGE LIBRARY
GOSHEN, INDIANA

thing is uncertain except the ultimate destruction of his hopes and the eventual realization of his fears. The most he can reasonably look forward to is that these things do not come too soon. Thus when Richard squanders a week's pay in 2 days it is not because, like an animal or a child, he is "present-time oriented", unaware of or unconcerned with his future. He does so precisely because he is aware of the future and the hopelessness of it all. ... Thus, apparent present-time concerns with consumption and indulgences – material and emotional – reflect a future time orientation. "I want mine right now" is ultimately a cry of despair, a direct response to the future as he sees it[4]' (1967, pp. 64–68).

The importance of conditions of life. To encourage greater delay of gratification, interventionists should focus on the conditions causing the 'hopelessness' and 'despair' in lower-income populations, rather than emphasizing the necessity of changing child-rearing patterns or simply saying that 'these people' have less intellectual potential because they cannot delay gratification. Other researchers have also noted that 'conditions of life' represented major causal factors contributing to parental practices and child development. MINTURN and LAMBERT [1964] interviewed mothers in six cultural settings (New England, Mexico, Philipines, Okinawa, India, and Kenya) and found that situational constraints in the mothers' immediate life space were primary determinants of their responses. HESS and SHIPMAN [1966] analyzed situational constraints among lower-income Americans and noted that 'a family in an urban ghetto has few choices to make with respect to such basic things as residence, occupation, and condition of housing, and on the minor points of choice that come with adequate discretionary income. A family with few opportunities to make choices among events that affect it is not likely to encourage the children to think of life as consisting of a wide range of behavioral options among which they must learn to discriminate' (p. 4).

The same authors [SHIPMAN and HESS, 1966] spoke specifically about language development: 'The lower-class mother's narrow range of alternatives is being conveyed to the child through language styles which convey her attitude of few options and little individual power, and this is now being reflected in the child's cognitive development' (p. 17).

GORDON [1969] reported specific data. He found that within the 'poverty group' the amount of verbal interaction directed toward an infant was related to the 'mother's view of her control of her destiny'. The extent to which an individual feels he has some control

---

[4] LIEBOW [1967] also pointed out that there is no intrinsic connection between 'present time' orientation and lower-class persons: 'Whenever people of whatever class have been uncertain, skeptical or downright pessimistic about the future, "I want mine right now" has been one of the characteristic responses... In wartime, especially, all classes tend to slough off conventional restraints on sexual and other behavior (i.e. become less able or less willing to defer gratification). And when inflation threatens, darkening the future, persons who formerly husbanded their resources with commendable restraint almost stampede one another rushing to spend their money... (Thus present-time orientation appears to be a situation-specific phenomenon rather than a part of the standard psychic equipment of cognitive lower-class man (1967, pp. 68–69).'

over his destiny is also related to a whole myriad of variables associated with educational achievement. COLEMAN *et al.* [1966] found that, among minority group students, this factor was the best predictor of academic success. Other research has demonstrated 'strong support for the hypotheses that the individual who has a strong belief that he can control his own destiny is likely to (a) be more alert to those aspects of the environment which provide useful information for his future behaviors; (b) take steps to improve his environmental position; (c) place greater value on skill or achievement reinforcements and be generally more concerned with his ability, particularly his failures; and (d) be resistive to subtle attempts to influence him' [ROTTER, 1966, p. 25]. There is little doubt that the realistic perception of the poor that they have little control over their lives leads not only to the 'hopelessness' and 'despair' observed by LIEBOW [1967], but also to less concern with education, and reduced academic success.

Interventionists must concern themselves with these social, economic and political realities of lower-class life and see the relations between these realities and indexes of parental behavior and intellectual development. Several interventionists have moved in this direction. SCHAEFER [1969] reported that 'current stresses and the absence of social support influence maternal hostility, abuse and neglect of the child'. He suggested that intervention programs hoping to change a mother's behavior toward her child needed to 'alleviate the stress and increase the support of mothers at the time the initial mother-child relationship is developed'.

Similarly, KAGAN [1969] spoke of the 'need for ecological change' to improve the conditions of life among lower-class populations. He emphasized that the interventionists needed to be sensitive to the 'communities belief as to what arrangements will help them', and that the changes should be directed toward facilitating the development of a 'sense of control over the future'.

Other researchers have come to the same conclusion. PAVENSTEDT [1967] reported that every member of her staff concurred 'in the conviction that far-reaching social and economic change must take place in order to fundamentally alter the lives of the families' they observed. STODOLSKY and LESSER [1968] suggested that intervention programs 'would probably be a lot more successful if we were to modify the conditions which probably lead to many of these (neglectful parental) behaviors; namely, lack of money and of access to jobs'. LIEBOW [1967] presented the most convincing argument: '...We do not have to see the problem in terms of breaking into a puncture proof circle, of trying to change values, of disrupting the lines of communication between parent and child so that parents cannot make children in their own image, thereby transmitting their culture inexorably, ad infinitum. No doubt, each generation does provide role models for each succeeding one. Of much greater importance for the possibilities of change, however, is the fact that many similarities between the lower-class Negro father and son (or mother and daughter) do not result from "cultural transmission" but from the fact that the son goes out and independently experiences the same failures, in the same areas, and for much the same reasons as his father. What appears as a dynamic, self-sustaining cultural process is, in part at least, a relatively simple piece of social machinery which turns out, in rather mechanical fashion, independently produced look-alikes. The problem is how to change the conditions which, by guaranteeing failure, cause the son to be made in the image of the father' (1967, p. 223).

Before we conclude that intervention programs will not work [JENSEN, 1969] we might want to consider some of these suggestions.

Roadblocks to change. Intervention programs which attempt to change the 'conditions of life', however, may encounter political opposition, simply because to change the conditions of life necessitates a wider distribution of power and wealth. While it is beyond the scope of the present discussion to closely examine the politics of poverty, it is necessary to understand why poverty may be difficult to eliminate.

Not all poor peoples share the characteristics which LEWIS [1965] calls the 'culture of poverty' or which researchers have labeled 'deprived'. LEWIS [1965] reported that these characteristics are found only among the poor people who occupy a 'marginal position in a class-stratified, highly individuated, capitalistic society' in which there is a 'lack of effective participation and integration of the poor in the major institutions of the larger society'. He reported, for example, that 'many of the primitive or preliterate peoples studies by anthropologists suffer from dire poverty which is the result of poor technology and/or poor natural resources, or of both, but they do not have the traits of the subculture of poverty. Indeed, they do not constitute a subculture because their societies are not highly stratified. In spite of their poverty they have a relatively integrated, satisfying and self-sufficient culture' (1965, p. XLVIII).

Where a 'culture of poverty' exists, however, the poor are less than poor: They are poor while others are rich, and they do not have the power to demand their 'fair share'. Thus, LEWIS [1965] aptly characterized the fight for equality in this country as a 'political power struggle' and pointed out that, rather than allowing poor people to effectively participate in society, many of those currently holding power 'emphasize the need for guidance and control to remain in the hands of the middle class...'. The culture of poverty will not be obliterated, however, until power is shared. The elimination of physical poverty *per se* may not be enough to eliminate the culture of poverty; more basic political changes may be necessary. Some might even argue that a political revolution is the only means of redistributing power and wealth, thus eliminating the culture of poverty. LEWIS [1965] noted that 'by creating basic structural changes in society, by redistributing wealth, by organizing the poor and giving them a sense of belonging, of power and of leadership, revolutions frequently succeed in abolishing some of the basic characteristics of the culture of poverty even when they do not succeed in abolishing poverty itself' (1965, p. LIII). To illustrate, LEWIS [1965] went on to report: 'On the basis of my limited experience in one socialist country – Cuba – and on the basis of my reading, I am inclined to believe that the culture of poverty does not exist in the socialist countries. After the Castro Revolution I found much less of the despair, apathy and hopelessness which are so diagnostic of urban slums in the culture of poverty. The people had a new sense of power and importance. They were armed and were given a doctrine which glorified the lower class as the hope of humanity' (1965, p. XLIX).

The purpose of this discussion is not necessarily to encourage political revolution, but rather to point out the complexities of attempting to understand the behavior of people who differ from us – culturally, financially, or any way. It is easier to think of these other people as 'groups', and more difficult to think of them as individuals who differ a great deal among themselves – just as members of our own group do. It is easier to think of them as wanting to be like us and needing us to help them; it is more difficult to reject the philosophy of the 'White Man's Burden' and allow people the freedom to retain life styles which differ from the ones we know. It is easy to blame people for what we have defined as their 'deficits', but more difficult to consider how we as a society might have contributed to the problems we have defined as 'theirs'.

Conclusion

We have attempted to point out how our assessments of intellectual development and of subcultural differences have been quite limited. Anthropologists have repeatedly warned that it is inappropriate to examine another culture through one's own experiential framework [CONKLIN, 1962; FRAKE, 1962], but psychologists have largely ignored these warnings. We would like to argue – not for a muzzling of scientific inquiry – but for an expansion of the perspectives from which scientific evidence is gathered. Western psychology has much to learn from studying nonliterate thinking and non-Western systems such as Zen. We must not continue to support the notion that the skills of white middle-class Americans are the only desireable skills or the best skills, or that white middle-class American child-rearing practices represent the model toward which all parents should strive.

Finally, we want to emphasize that we are not suggesting that there is no such thing as a deficit, or that all interventions in the developmental process are ill-conceived. But, we have indicated that deprivation is largely in the eyes of the beholder, which suggests that interventions should proceed on the basis of a much wider knowledge of consequences of different sets of experiences than we now have. Given this limited scope of our present areas of inquiry, and given that we may be about to enter a period of crisis for our species [TOFFLER, 1970], we – as a scientific community – should be wary of any programs which might tend to narrow the field of human variability available to us.

References

ABRAMOWICZ, M. and KASS, E.H.: Pathogenesis and prognosis of prematurity. New Engl. J. Med. *275:* 878 (1966).

American College Dictionary (Random House, New York 1959).

ARAI, S.; ISHIKAWA, J. et TOSHIMA, K.: Developpement psychomoteur des enfants Japonais. Rev. Neuropsychiat. infant. *6:* 262–269 (1958); cited by CAUDILL and WEINSTEIN (1969).

BARATZ, J.C. and SHUY, R.W. (eds.): Teaching black children to read (Center for Applied Linguistics, Washington 1969).

BARATZ, S.S. and BARATZ, J.C.: Early childhood intervention. The social science base of institutional racism. Harv. educ. Rev. *40:* 29–50 (1970).

BERNSTEIN, B.: Language and social class. Brit. J. Sociology *11:* 271–276 (1960).

BERNSTEIN, B.: Social class and linguistic development. A theory of social learning; in HALSEY, FLOUD and ANDERSON Education, economy and society, pp. 288–314 (Free Press, Glencoe 1961).

BIRREN, J.E. and HESS, R.: Influences of biological, psychological, and social deprivations on learning and performance; in Perspectives on human deprivation. Department of Health, Education and Welfare, Washington, pp. 105–217 (1968).

BLURTON JONES, N.G. and KONNER, M.J.: Knowledge of animal behavior among the Kalahari Desert Bushmen. Department of Psychology and Social Relations, Harvard University (unpubl. manuscript, 1972).

BROCKMAN, L.M. and RICCIUTI, H.N.: Severe protein-calorie malnutrition and cognitive development in infancy and early childhood. Develop. Psychol. 4: 312–319 (1971).

BRUNER, J.; OLVER, R., and GREENFIELD, P.: Studies in cognitive growth (Wiley, New York 1966).

CAUDILL, W. and WEINSTEIN, H.: Maternal care and infant behavior in Japanese and American urban middle class families. National Institute of Mental Health, Bethesda (unpubl. manuscript, 1966).

CAUDILL, W. and WEINSTEIN, H.: Maternal care and infant behavior in Japan and America. Psychiatry 32: 12–43 (1969).

CHANDLER, B.J. and ERICKSON, F.D.: Sounds of society. A demonstration program in group inquiry. Department of Health, Education, and Welfare; Office of Education, Bureau of Research, Washington (1968).

CLEAVER, E.: Soul on ice (McGraw-Hill, New York 1968).

COLE, M.; GAY, J.; GLICK, J.A., and SHARP, D.W.: The cultural context of learning and thinking (Basic Books, New York 1971).

COLEMAN, J.S.; CAMPBELL, E.Q.; HOBSON, C.J.; McPARTLAND, J.; MOOD, A.M.; WEINFELD, F.D., and YORK, R.L.: Equality of educational opportunity (United States Office of Education, Washington 1966).

CONKLIN, H.C.: The ethnographic study of cognitive systems; in Anthropology and human behavior (Anthropological Society of Washington, Washington 1962).

DILLARD, J.L.: Black English (Random House, New York 1972).

ELKIN, A.P.: The Australian aborigines (Angus & Robertson, Sydney 1964).

FANON, F.: The wretched of the earth (Grove Press, New York 1968).

FANTINI, M.D.: Beyond cultural deprivation and compensatory education. Psychiat. Soc. Sci. Rev. 3: 6–13 (1969).

FJELLMAN, J.S.: The myth of primitive mentality. A study of semantic acquisition and modes of categorization in Akamba children of south central Kenya; dissertation Stanford (1971).

FOSTER, H.L.: Dialect-lexicon and listening comprehension; dissertation New York (1969).

FOSTER, H.L.: Foster's Jive Lexicon Analogies Test. Series II. Office of Teacher Education, State University of New York at Buffalo (unpubl. report, 1970).

FRAKE, C.O.: The ethnographic study of cognitive systems; in Anthropology and human behavior (Anthropological Society of Washington, Washington 1962).

GORDON, I.J.: Early child stimulation through parent education. Department of Health, Education and Welfare; Children's Bureau, Social and Rehabilitation Service, Washington (1969).

GROSS, M.: Learning readiness in two Jewish groups (Center for Urban Education, New York 1967).

HESS R.D. and SHIPMAN, V.C.: Maternal attitude toward the school and the role of pupil. Some social class comparisons. Proc. Conf. on Curriculum and Teaching in Depressed Urban Areas, New York 1966.

HILLSON, M.: The disadvantaged child. Community ment. Hlth J. *6:* 81–83 (1970).

JENSEN, A.R.: How much can we boost IQ and scholastic achievement. Harv. educ. Rev. *39:* 1–123 (1969).

KAGAN, J.: Information processing in the child; in MUSSEN, CONGER and KAGAN Readings in child development and personality, pp. 313–323 (Harper & Row, New York 1965).

KAGAN, J.: Social class and academic progress. An analysis and suggested solution strategies. Proc. Meet. amer. Ass. Advancement of Science, Boston 1969.

KAUNDA, K.: A humanist in Zambia (Abingdon Press, New York 1966).

KNOBLOCK, H. and PASAMANICK, B.: Mental subnormality. New Engl. J. Med. *266:* 1092–1097 (1962).

KONNER, M.J.: Aspects of the developmental ethology of a foraging people; in BLURTON JONES Ethological studies of child behaviour (Cambridge Univ. Press, New York 1971).

KONNER, M.J.: Maternal care, infant behavior, and development among the Zhun/twa Bushmen; in LEE Studies of Zhun/twa hunter-gatherers (in press).

KRAUSS, R.M. and ROTTER, G.S.: Communication abilities of children as a function of status and age. Merrill-Palmer Quart. *14:* 161–174 (1968).

LABOV, W.: Some sources of reading problems for Negro speakers of non-standard English; in FRAZIER New directions in elementary English (National Council of Teachers of English, Champaign 1967).

LAUGHLIN, W.S.: Hunting. An integrating biobehavior system and its evolutionary importance; in LEE and DE VORE Man the hunter, pp. 304–320 (Aldine, Chicago 1968).

LEHMER, M.: Navajos want their own schools. San Francisco Examiner and Chronicle, December 14, 4 (1969).

LEVI-STRAUSS, C.: Totemism (Beacon Press, Boston 1963).

LEVI-STRAUSS, C.: The savage mind (Univ. of Chicago Press, Chicago 1966).

LEVI-STRAUSS, C.: The elementary structures of kinship (Beacon Press, Boston 1969).

LEWIS, O.: LaVida. A Puerto Rican family in the culture of poverty (Random House, New York 1965).

LIEBOW, E.: Tally's corner. A study of Negro streetcorner men (Little Brown, Boston 1967).

MACCOBY, M. and MODIANO, N.: On culture and equivalence I; in BRUNER, OLVER and GREENFIELD Studies in cognitive growth, pp. 257–269 (Wiley, New York 1966).

MADSEN, M.C.: Developmental and cross-cultural differences in the cooperative and competitive behavior of young children. J. Cross-Cultural Psychol. *2:* 365–371 (1971).

MAILER, N.: Advertisements for myself (Putnam, New York 1959).

MEAD, M.: An investigation of the thought of primitive children, with special reference to animism. J. roy. anthrop. Inst. *62:* 173–190 (1932); reprinted in HUNT (ed.) Personalities and cultures (Natural History Press, New York 1967).

MINTURN, L. and LAMBERT, W.W.: Mothers of six cultures (Wiley, New York 1964).

PAVENSTEDT, E. (ed.): The drifters (Little Brown, Boston 1967).

REBELSKY, F. and ABELES, G.: Infancy in Holland and in the United States. Proc. Soc. for Research in Child Development, Santa Monica 1969.

RIEGEL, K.F.: Influence of economic and political ideologies on the development of developmental psychology. Psychol. Bull. *78:* 129–141 (1972).

ROTTER, J.B.: Generalized expectancies for internal versus external control of reinforcement. Psychol. Monogr. *80:* 1–28 (1966).

RYAN, W.: Blaming the victim (Pantheon, New York 1971).

SCHAEFER, E.S.: Need for early and continuing education. Proc. Meet. amer. Ass. Advancement of Science, Boston 1969.

SHIPMAN, V.C. and HESS, R.D.: Early experiences in the socialization of cognitive modes in children. A study of urban Negro families. Proc. Meet Conf. Family and Society Merrill-Palmer Institute, Detroit 1966.

SROUFE, L.A.: A methodological and philosophical critique of intervention-oriented research. Develop. Psychol. *2:* 140–145 (1970).

STEWART, W.A.: Sociolinguistic factors in the history of American Negro dialects. The Florida FL Reporter, vol. 5 II (1967).

STEWART, W.A.: Linguistic and conceptual deprivation – fact or fancy? Proc. Meet. Soc. Res. Child Development, Santa Monica 1969a.

STEWART, W.A.: On the use of Negro dialect in the teaching of reading; in BARATZ and SHUY Teaching black children to read, pp. 156–219 (Center for Applied Linguistics, Washington 1969b).

STODOLSKY, S. and LESSER, G.: Learning patterns in the disadvantaged; in CHESS and THOMAS Annual progress in child psychiatry and child development, pp. 224–272 (Brunner/Mazel, New York 1968).

TOFFLER, A.: Future shock (Random House, New York 1970).

WATTS, A.: The way of Zen (Random House, New York 1957).

WILLIAMS, R.L. and RIVERS, L.W.: The use of standard versus non-standard English in the administration of group tests to black children. Department of Black studies, Washington University, St. Louis (unpubl. manuscript, 1972).

Request reprints from: Dr. S.R. TULKIN, Department of Psychology, State University of New York at Buffalo, *Buffalo, NY 14226* (USA)

Human Develop. *16:* 53–60 (1973)

From Each According to His Abilities:
The Role of Effort in a Moral Society[1]

B. WEINER

University of California, Los Angeles, Calif.

Abstract. Achievement behavior is determined by 'try' (effort) as well as 'can' (ability). Experimentation reveals that individuals do perceive that trying is a central determinant of outcome. Further, achievement evaluation is, in part, based upon the amount of effort expenditure, independent of outcome. Thus, achievement evaluation has moral components. In addition, there is a similarity in the development of achievement and moral judgments, with both progressing from objective to subjective factors as the basis for evaluation. Basing achievement evaluation upon subjective causes is the foundation of KARL MARX's conception of a communistic state. It is contended that KARL MARX and JEAN PIAGET have similar conceptions of social and personal development. By focusing so much attention on the measurement of ability, psychologists have neglected the subjective determinants of achievement striving and achievement evaluation. We must consider the moral aspects of achievement, and turn 'from each according to his ability' toward the establishment of a moral society.

Key Words
Achievement evaluation
Achievement motivation
Causal ascriptions
Communism
Effort
Moral development
Moral society

We are all aware that the testing of intellective functions has played a central role in the history of psychology and has had great social value. The rationale guiding mental testing is quite simple. It is assumed that ability influences achievement outcomes, and is presumably the most important contributor to achievement performance. For any given task, as ability increases, the probability of successfully completing that task is assumed to increase. In a similar manner, it is reasoned that with increasing ability one 'can' successfully perform more difficult tasks. It is, therefore, quite logical

[1] This paper was written while the author was supported by grant GS–35216 from the National Science Foundation. Appreciation is extended to Dr. DANA BRAMEL for his suggestions.

to seek information pertaining to a person's ability level to aid in predicting
school performance, occupational success, and so forth.

But the phenomenology of achievement performance recognizes determinants of outcome in addition to the conceptually stable factors of ability
and task difficulty. In skill-related situations, the most important of the
changeable or unstable factors that influence performance is *effort*. My goal
in this paper is to document the role that effort plays as a perceived determinant of achievement performance and achievement evaluation. This will
lead to a cognitive-developmental analysis of achievement motivation, and
some proposed similarities between the development of achievement striv-
ings and the development of morality. I will conclude by arguing that a
moral social system, as envisioned by KARL MARX, and a moral individual,
as characterized by JEAN PIAGET, acknowledge the inadequacies of employing ability rather than effort (intent) ascriptions as the basis for social evaluation. We must, therefore, turn our attention from the measurement of
ability toward the analysis of intention and the promotion of effort.

The Naive Analysis of Effort

The naive analysis of action, or the psychology of motivation as perceived
by the 'man on the street', specifies 'can' and 'try' as the major determinants of achievement outcomes [HEIDER, 1958]. Can is in part a function of
ability level, while try reflects the individual's expenditure of effort. Although
at most tasks some minimal level of both ability *and* effort are perceived as
necessary to attain a goal, in general these two factors are perceived as compensatory and are *sufficient* causes of a positive outcome. One hears a student professing, for example, that 'I am smart enough to receive an "A" in
this easy course without studying' or 'I know that if I practice enough I
can win, even though 'I have little skill'.

In a series of studies we have examined the perceived relationships between ability and outcome and effort expenditure and outcome. The experimental procedure is straightforward. Individuals are described as having
various degrees of ability and as expending various amounts of effort. Subjects must then predict the level of outcome of these hypothetical persons.
More specifically, in one experiment students were described as high, medium, or low in ability, and as high, medium, or low in 'trying'. The subjects
then specified the score on an exam (1–100) that each of the nine types of
students (3 levels of ability × 3 levels of effort) would attain. The data from

such studies clearly reveal that, within extended ranges, ability and effort are perceived as compensatory; extra effort can overcome the handicap of low ability, and vice versa. In addition, effort often is perceived as a more important determinant of outcome than is ability. The differential main effect stressing the importance of effort is displayed by children as young as six years of age. Of course, this does not mean that effort *is* a more important influence on performance than is ability. But effort frequently is *perceived* as having greater weight, and it may not be unreasonable to believe that such perceptions have some degree of veridicality.

Achievement Evaluation

Do the perceived 'can' and 'try' determinants of action differentially influence evaluations of achievement performance? The data indicate that the answer to this question is an unequivocal 'yes'. Again a very simple experimental paradigm has been employed to explore this question. Subjects are asked to pretend that they are teachers, dispensing rewards and punishments to their pupils. The pupils are described in terms of their level of ability (high or low), effort expenditure (high or low), and their outcome on an exam (ranging from clear success to clear failure). All possible combinations of these three factors are appraised. For example, a pupil is evaluated who is high in ability, low in effort, having a moderate failure on an exam. The rewards extend from +1 to +5 points, and the punishments from –1 to –5 points.

The results of one representative investigation by WEINER and KUKLA [1970] are shown in figure 1. Figure 1 reveals that outcome significantly affects evaluation – success is generally rewarded while failure usually is punished. In addition, effort is clearly an evaluative determinant. High-perceived effort gives rise to more reward and less punishment than low-perceived effort. Finally, perceived ability also influences rewards and punishments, but in a manner opposite to what might be expected. *Low*-perceived ability is rewarded more and punished less than high-perceived ability. This rather strange result apparently is due to the fact that when one tries hard and overcomes an ability deficit, he or she is especially rewarded. The reader surely can recall the admiration given to a person who surmounted a physical handicap and accomplished a difficult feat, such as completing a marathon race. On the other hand, the person with high ability who does not utilize his capacities is especially punished for failure. Introspect about your affect

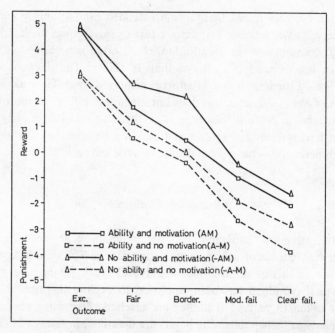

Fig. 1. Evaluation (reward and punishment) as a function of perceived pupil ability, effort expenditure and examination outcome (college sample) [from WEINER and KUKLA, 1970].

towards those bright graduate students who are not working, and are handing in poor exams! It is as though it were *immoral* to let one's potential ('can') go to 'waste'.

The Development of Effort Structures

The finding that achievement evaluation among adults is mediated by causal ascriptions to effort calls attention to a similarity between achievement and moral judgments. It has been documented by PIAGET [1932] and others that, among adults, the intent of the actor is the main determinant of moral evaluation. Perceived intent and perceived effort, the respective foundations of moral and achievement evaluation, are ascriptions to the person, and are believed to be subject to volitional control. In the light of the similarity in the determinants of adult evaluation, one might speculate that achievement appraisal follows the same cognitive-developmental sequence as moral judgment. It has been shown that the determinants of

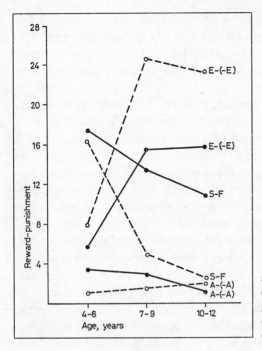

Fig. 2. Achievement (●) evaluation and moral (○) judgment (amount of reward or punishment given) as a function of ability, effort or intent, and outcome among children ages 4–12 years.

moral judgment shift from *objective outcome* to *subjective intent* with increasing maturity. Does this same sequence characterize achievement evaluation?

To test this question the experiment illustrated in figure 1 was administered to children ages 4–12 years. To simplify the procedure somewhat, only two levels of outcome (success or failure) were used. Thus, each child made 8 achievement judgments (2 levels of ability × 2 levels of effort × 2 levels of outcome). In addition, a second experimental condition was included, portraying a moral rather than an achievement situation. A story was related to the subjects in which a young child was lost and was seeking help to return home. An older child was characterized as knowing or not knowing the correct directions (ability), and as wanting or not wanting to help (intent). In addition, the lost child either found or did not find his way home (outcome). The subjects again judged all eight possible combinations of ability, effort, and outcome. For example, reward or punishment points were assigned to an older child who knew the directions, did not want to help, and the younger child did not get home, etc.

The results of one such study are shown in figure 2. The figure includes only the overall main effects of the three evaluative determinants. That is,

rewards and punishments for success are contrasted with appraisal for failure (S–F); ability is contrasted with lack of ability (A–[–A]); and effort
(intent) is contrasted with lack of effort (E–[–E]). The dependent variable is
the relative appraisal (reward minus punishment points) administered by
the subjects.

Looking first at the morality data, it can be observed that among the
younger children objective outcome (whether the lost child does or does not
get home) is the main determinant of moral judgment. That is, reward is
dispensed if the child gets home, while punishment generally is given if the
child does not return home. The difference between the appraisal for a positive outcome (success) and the appraisal for a negative outcome (failure)
(S–F) is relatively great among children prior to the age of 7 years. But by
the age of 7 years, perceived intent is the information most used to determine morality. Good intent is rewarded and bad intent is punished, regardless of the outcome of the action. Indeed, after 9 years of age intent is the
only significant determinant of moral evaluation in this hypothetical situation. These data are quite consistent with the observations of PIAGET.

Turning attention next to the achievement data, a similar developmental
sequence can be observed. Younger children believe that success and failure
are the main evaluative factors in achievement settings. If one succeeds, he
or she should be rewarded; if one fails, he or she should be punished. But
by the age of 7 years effort emerges as a more important determinant of
achievement appraisal than outcome. Trying is rewarded and not trying is
relatively punished. In neither the moral nor the achievement situation is
the level of ability predictive of social rewards. However, from the data
reported in figure 1 in which college students were the subjects, we would
expect lack of ability to exert a positive evaluative influence with still further
cognitive development.[2]

A Moral Society

We have seen that achievement and moral evaluation follow similar
developmental sequences, with effort or intent replacing or supplementing
outcome as the main factor in social evaluation. The idea that achievements

[2] Recent data we have collected indicates that, with increasing age, outcome again
becomes a more important determinant of achievement evaluation than effort, although
effort remains a highly significant influence on appraisal. This change or regression in the
use of evaluative structures is believed to be due to our society's emphasis upon products
rather than intents (see WEINER and PETER, in press).

should be evaluated according to some criteria other than outcome is not new. It is the very essence of KARL MARX's conception of a just society. In *The Critique of the Gotha Program*, MARX [1875] outlines the dynamics of social change and social progress. To summarize briefly, MARX contends that progress in society comes about through conflict. Using the analogy of the dialectic method of discourse, he argues that the forces of production of society repeatedly come into conflict with the social order. Out of this clash of forces social change *(synthesis)* emerges. The evolution in political form and economic structure is conceived as an inevitable historical process. Further, historical development proceeds in discrete stages, with each new stage determined by the prior conditions existing in society.

The final stage of society, communism, thus springs from the societies that precede it. The immediately prior social stages are first capitalism and then socialism. As conceptualized by MARX, these two economic forms differ primarily in the extent to which the means of production, and hence surplus goods, are in the hands of individuals *versus* society. However, in both social systems labor continues to exist, and social reward is based upon how much each person is able to contribute: 'The same quantity of labor which he has given society in one form [work] he receives back in another [income]' [MARX, 1875, p. 118]. But this allocation of rewards, based upon outcome or productivity, is not moral or humanistic, according to MARX. Individuals differ in their capacities or capabilities, i.e. in whether they 'can' or 'cannot'. Further, because of factors such as family size, some persons require more goods than others. Thus, equality in theory gives way to inequality in practice. In reaching the true communistic state, the distribution of wealth progresses 'from each according to his abilities, to each according to his needs' [MARX, 1875, p. 119]. Every member of society contributes what he is able, and is given in return what he needs. The social character produced by the economic change results in the idle individual being a rare and abnormal exception; every individual theoretically will expend maximal effort for the social good.

Marx and Piaget: A Convergence

It is evident from the above discussion that both MARX and PIAGET postulate invariant sequences of change through which the individual and society must progress before a final 'moral' stage is reached. In addition, both MARX and PIAGET postulate a similar developmental progression.

Social evaluation initially is based upon objective outcomes, but with increased growth appraisal is dependent upon subjective factors, such as effort and intent. Achievement appraisal in a Marxian system is, therefore, a moral appraisal.

MARX, although writing prior to PIAGET, apparently has formulated a recapitulation theory of social history. The evolution of society recapitulates the moral development of the individual. Paradoxically, once the final social state has been reached, it would appear *as if* the development of the child were recapitulating the growth of society. This maturational sequence would approximate the familiar 'ontogeny recapitulates phylogeny', which was accepted by PIAGET.

What Have we to Learn?

By concentrating so much of our attention on mental capacities, and by considering only the rewards of 'each according to his abilities', psychologists have neglected the role of intent and volition as determinants of achievement evaluation and achievement performance. We have not created Headstart programs that teach affective (motivational) development. We have not performed job analyses that specify the compensatory effects of motivation. We have not alerted individuals to their own value systems. That is, we have overlooked the *moral* aspects of achievement evaluation, and focused upon the building and analysis of intellective functioning. Perhaps it is time to redress this imbalance, and proceed in our thoughts and in our actions '*from* each according to his abilities', toward the creation of a just and a moral society.

References

HEIDER, F.: The psychology of interpersonal relations (Wiley, New York 1958).

MARX, K.: The critique of the Gotha Program (1875); in MARX and ENGELS Basic writings on politics and philosophy, pp. 112–132 (Anchor Books, Garden City 1959).

PIAGET, J.: The moral judgment of the child (1932) (Free Press, New York 1948).

WEINER, B. and KUKLA, A.: An attributional analysis of achievement motivation. J. personal. social psychol. *15:* 1–20 (1970).

WEINER, B. and PETER, N.: A cognitive-developmental analysis of achievement and moral judgments. Develop. Psychol. (in press).

Request reprints from: Dr. B. WEINER, Department of Psychology, University of California, *Los Angeles, CA 90024* (USA)

Human Develop. *16:* 61–73 (1973)

Piaget, IQ and the Nature-Nurture Controversy

H. G. Furth

Catholic University of America, Washington, D.C.

Abstract. PIAGET's concepts of experience and subject-object interaction are clarified. Species-specific developmental experiences that are common to all people are distinguished from particular learned experiences on which individual differences are based. Four basic assumptions of IQ tests – age constancy, scholastic validity, standard environment and performance sufficiency – are examined and found alien to PIAGET's theory. In conclusion, heredity is not a concept that can be statistically separated from environment and thus from PIAGET's standpoint the nature-nurture controversy is devoid of meaning.

Key Words
Environment
Experience
Heredity
IQ test
Individual differences
Interaction
Maturation
PIAGET's theory

PIAGET's theory of intellectual development is frequently interpreted as being an interactionist and maturational stage theory. This interpretation can be defended but requires an understanding of the words 'interaction' and 'maturation' rather different from their traditional use. One speaks of two factors interacting when these two factors have a clearly defined existence and contribute in differing proportion to the existence of a third factor. In this manner the traditional nature-nurture question is approached. Statistics are used to arrive at a numerical estimate of the relative importance of either innate or environmental factors on intellectual development.

One may legitimately ask what stand PIAGET's theory could take on this question. From his insistence on the internal regulatory mechanisms of development it would be easy to conclude that his theory attributes an overriding role to innate and hereditary conditions. Similarly, when the word maturation is applied to a theory of development, the stress is on the innate side of the supposed contributing factors. PIAGET's conception of developmental stages could then be readily seen in the light of an internal physiological mechanism to which environmental contributions are almost incidental.

It is the purpose of this paper to show first that the suggested interpretations of PIAGET's theory are quite inadequate and misleading. After these preliminary considerations we shall concern ourselves with PIAGET's position vis-à-vis three basic questions in the nature-nurture controversy, namely, individual differences, standard tests and heredity.

Experience and Interaction in Piaget's Theory

First, one cannot in PIAGET's view neatly separate organism and environment as two preexisting entities the interaction of which would lead to the development of human intelligence. Second, the stages of which PIAGET speaks are not physiological mechanisms but mechanisms of human behavior. The condition for their appearance is not, or is not merely, the maturation of physiological organs but primarily human behavior in a human environment. The repetition of the words human in the preceding phrase is to underline the type of behavior and environment that is required and the common bond that links these two notions. In other words, not just any existence or activity leads to stage-characteristic development but activities that are species-specific in a biological sense, that is in our case, activities to which evolution has adapted the human person and his environment.

In line with PIAGET's thinking human behavior in all its varieties can be considered from two angles. First, as representative of common human capacities of knowing and, second, as representative of particular skills and individually varying contingencies. For instance, an infant who can walk purposefully from one place to another in his immediate neighborhood demonstrates at the same time the common sensorimotor mechanism of 'knowing to walk' and the particular knowing of his immediate whereabouts. Depending on one's interest, one can focus on the particular learning aspect of this achievement in which case the particular contingencies of the environment play a crucial role, or one can focus on the common species-specific aspect of walking behavior in which case one ignores the particular and individualistic components and considers only the common components of the environment, e.g., gravity, stable physical objects, visual and tactual cues, etc.

Take as another example of a more theoretical behavior children's comprehension of combinatorial properties. A child may have blocks of three colors in front of him and make pairs or triplets of blocks of different colors. To understand a sequence of two or three different items is easy enough for a three- or four-year-old. To learn to name colors or to identify some other items that could be arranged in a sequence, say, a spoon, a fork, a knife, is also an easy achievement. These identifications presuppose of course among other things particular contingencies to which the individual child was exposed. But it takes the further experience of a number of years until the child comprehends combinatorial ordering in a systematic manner, e.g., blue blue, blue yellow, blue red, yellow blue, yellow yellow, etc. This ordering is not a thing which the child can find in his environment; on the contrary, it is what PIAGET calls a reflective feedback from the child's own actions on the environment. The experience of ordering which the child has – actively doing the ordering himself or observing it in another person's doing – can be described from two viewpoints. Either as a physical or simple experience mainly responsible for particular learning as exemplified above, or as a logical-mathematical experience that leads in the typical seven- to nine-year-old child to a basic understanding of sequential properties. Consequently, PIAGET would propose that experience with the environment is indeed needed for the acquisition of combinatorial thinking, but the crucial factor is the developmental – PIAGET calls it logical-mathematical – aspect of the experience that is a reflective feedback from the child's own activities and not the physical aspect of the experience that focuses on the physical properties of the environment.

These examples illustrate that the preconditions of developmental stages are much more than either maturation of physiological tissue – even though it may be a necessary factor – or becoming acquainted with information that only the physical or social environment can supply; although both of these factors are obviously necessary. In PIAGET's theory the critical variable is developmental experience with its attendant reflective feedback. This is the immediate causal factor of human intelligence and is as common and species-specific as any other biological characteristic of human persons.

These three factors – physiological maturation, learning of particular environmental information and developmental experience – are not separately existing processes or behaviors. Rather they are three interrelated aspects of one concrete reality, namely, the growing child in his cognitive activity. Just as cognition is a partial aspect of the child's total functioning which includes motivational and dynamic aspects, similarly intelligence (or preforms of intelligence) according to PIAGET is a partial aspect that enters into all cognitive activities at all stages of development.

Take the words subjective and objective in relation to organism and environment. For traditional positivistic philosophy there is no doubt how the four words should be paired: objective goes with the environment and subjective with the organism. The objective is the facts of which the 'real' world is made, whereas the subjective is the contribution of the individual who has not yet learned the objective facts. Development in this view is a learning of these facts and a decrease of subjectivity comes about in direct proportion to the intake of objectivity.

PIAGET, however, points out two meanings of the word subjective. One meaning links the word to what is individualistic in behavior, in an idiosyncratic and deforming sense that contrasts with the eventually necessary perspective of adult logic; the other meaning is almost the opposite, namely that component of the person that contributes to the construction of the afore-mentioned perspective. This component is nothing else but human intelligence conceived as the biological common basis that makes men thinking human beings. Thus PIAGET studies in intelligence what is common or species-specific to man. Objectivity, far from being found in the outside world, is the product of this common subjective contribution in contact with the common environment. A child fails in objective thinking, not because he has not learned enough objective facts from outside, but because he has not yet constructed powerful enough mechanisms of thinking by means of which he can have a socially common measure and criterion of objectivity. For PIAGET, objectivity is not present at the beginning of intellectual development in the form of environmental specifications but at the end of the development in the form of internal subject-produced criteria of objectivity.

The biologically common environment is but the counterpart of the common subjective in all human beings. Indeed, biology has never been able to separate the two poles of organism and environment since one is adapted to the other through evolution. These two poles are not independent entities the interaction of which produces intelligence. Rather they should be considered as mutually related in such a way that as one changes the other changes. In the case of human development, the common environment, in and on which the subject acts, is to be conceived as dependent on the mechanisms of thinking; these the subject continually constructs in the course of and as a consequence of acting. In a similar vein one can assert that behavior and the underlying mechanisms of behaving and thinking are dependent on the common environment to which human beings are biologically adapted.

Consequently this position cannot be called maturationist or interactionist in the traditional sense. The fact of behavioral experience within a human environment as an obligatory component in individual development is contrary to the usual notion of maturation as opposed to personal experience. The mutual dependence and reciprocal construction of the subject as knower and the environment as objectively known is inconsistent with the usual meaning of the interaction of two presumably given factors.

Individual Differences

With this as background we turn to three basic problems closely related to the nature-nurture controversy. First there is the question of individual differences. PIAGET's theory apparently does not take account of differences but rather focuses on what is common and biologically characteristic in the functioning of human intelligence. He takes seriously the proposition that one has first to understand the basic nature of a phenomenon before studying its range of variations. PIAGET's investigations are not unlike those of ethologists who seek to discover species-specific characteristics of behavior about certain animals. These investigators know full well that innumerable pre- or postnatal conditions can alter certain typical behavior patterns but, nonetheless, no scholar would deny that there are behavior patterns as characteristic of a species as physiological or anatomical features.

The place for individual differences in PIAGET's theory was indicated above with the distinction between two aspects of experience and two aspects of environments. Developmental experience with its reflective feedback and the common environment are critical for the development of the general human capacity for knowing, i.e. intelligence. Particular physical experiences and particular environments plus, one may add, particular skills or deficiencies in instrumental modalities (e.g., so-called creative talent in special domains or sensorial deficiencies) are aspects of knowing that are susceptible to wide individual differences. These differences are then manifested in the learning of practical or symbolic skills. Moreover, since these two aspects of knowing cannot be dissociated, the distinction although theoretically clear and necessary is not one that can be externally manipulated or observed. It is, in the final analysis, a question of perspective: In any behavior we can focus on one or the other aspect. PIAGET has coined the distinction between operative and figurative knowing where operative refers to the action and transforming aspect of knowing and figurative to the configurational and static aspect of knowing. One can then link up the phrase 'operative knowing' with the basic common development of intelligence from birth to adulthood. This operative development provides the framework of behavioral and thinking mechanisms which make possible the learning of particular figurative content. Thus, while PIAGET has concentrated his interest on what is common in human intelligence, there is ample opportunity in his theoretical setting to look for individual differences.

Assumptions of IQ tests

The second question addresses if not the core of the nature-nurture controversy, at least its indispensable tool, namely, the intelligence test. How is the intelligence of PIAGET's theory related to the intelligence of IQ tests? PIAGET's answer is unambiguous: There is only a weak or superficial relation; essentially IQ intelligence and what PIAGET calls operative intelligence, are two different things. One can put the situation more mildly by saying that PIAGET's theory and intelligence tests look at the same phenomena, but look at them from two different perspectives. This difference is no accidental historical coincidence but rather the outcome of a purposeful divergence from a common scientific tradition. If PIAGET's theory owes a historical debt to the psychological and scientific atmosphere before him, this is only as natural for his as for any theory. But it is remarkable that BINET's influence for German and English psychology has been almost uniquely identified with his methodology for measuring intelligence; whereas in PIAGET's case BINET's theoretical and experimental work remained preponderant. The ironic result was that PIAGET's psychological career in fact started in the laboratory of BINET's collaborator SIMON on research connected with standardization of some verbal test items. But PIAGET found himself much more interested in the thinking mechanisms underlying right and wrong answers of children than simply tabulating the frequency of different kinds of responses.

Four assumptions are commonly accepted by all types of standardized IQ tests and all of them would be severely questioned by PIAGET. I call them here the assumptions of (1) age constancy, (2) scholastic validity, (3) standard environment, and (4) performance sufficiency. Assumptions 1 and 2 are prerequisite for the statistical treatment of IQ scores. Assumption 1 identifies chronological speed of achievement with greater intelligence and assumption 2 accepts scholastic success as a valid criterion for IQ test scores. PIAGET admits and documents a much greater age variability than would be acceptable for measurement purposes. His own observations have shown PIAGET that, e.g., responses characteristic of the most advanced stage in physical thinking can be found in one child of 6 years and another child of 15 years [PIAGET, 1969, p. 202]. In all his work one encounters data attesting to a large span of years in which stage-typical responses were observed. Thus, for the drawing of a tube that somersaults from the edge of the table to the floor PIAGET and INHELDER [1971, p. 127] report 25% correct anticipations at 4 years up to 70% correct at 8 years; on the correct intersection of two classes [INHELDER and PIAGET, 1969, p. 178] the percentage rises from 15 at ages 5–6 to 82 at ages 9–10. Not only that, PIAGET [1969, p. 205] observes without surprise that the same child thinks at a higher substage in connection with the concept of life and at a lower substage with the related concept of consciousness.

Nowhere does PIAGET pretend that stages of thinking reached in one domain will necessarily be found in the thinking of the same person in another domain. Nor does he consider stages as linked to an absolute chronological age; when PIAGET mentions ages for purposes of illustration he speaks at the same time of the observed range of variations and the possibility that in a different environment and with different schooling some other age range may be discovered. Stages for PIAGET mean nothing else than a lawful and logically consistent succession of one stage necessarily before another as children grow up into adults. However, even though operative stages are lawfully ordered and constitute common human acquisitions, they have a personal history of slow and gradual preparation, elaboration and final stability.[1]

There is ample evidence that all healthy persons in all societies and ranks of life reach the stage of concrete operations. A like assertion cannot be made with equal confidence for formal thinking. PIAGET is rightly cautious on this point. The closer a person is to adulthood the more likely is it that individual and particularly also sociocultural preferences and opportunities have a decisive influence on the content and manner in which a person's intelligence is used. PIAGET [1972] suggests that some type of formal think-

[1] In addition to stable inter-individual differences and in contrast to a model of cumulative learning, Piaget's view respects the normal variability of the developing child whose performance during periods of transition rises and falls. This intra-individual variability makes difficult reliable measurement of the long-range growth of operative development.

ing is likely to be observed in all cultures where adults are seriously engaged in a speciality of their concern (e.g., building of ships, administration of law). We all know, moreover, that in some domains we ourselves apply a higher level of thinking than in others and in this respect great individual differences even within a homogeneous subgroup of society are the rule rather than the exception.

The reader may by now be rightly impressed by the ample indications for individual variations in a theory which he perhaps suspected to be a rigid, internally controlled clockwork. But then, he may ask, of what use is PIAGET's theory if the intelligence he speaks of does not proceed in a statistically standardized fashion? Perhaps this is not the place to expose the inadequacy of the scientific perspective which underlies this kind of question. Instead I would like to present PIAGET's reply to the usefulness of learning machines [PIAGET, 1970, p. 78], and apply it to IQ tests. If IQ tests are found to be highly correlated with and, therefore, predictive of scholastic success, this merely shows something about the present aim and character of the schools; he would say further that schools have indeed much to do with the things that IQ tests sample, but they have not much to do with creative and challenging thinking. Consider how absurd it would be if a physical activities teacher who spent day after day in appropriate and challenging activities would require some outside expert to evaluate a child's potential on a one-shot basis. Apart from the isolated case where medical advice is needed for an exceptional condition, would you not wonder what this teacher had been doing with the child all along? If educators are eager to have IQ scores on a child, one can only conclude that ordinary classroom activities do not give them good opportunities to evaluate the child's intelligence. In short, IQ tests are valid indicators of scholastic performance to a degree to which operative evaluation in PIAGET's sense could never lay claim. But this fact may turn to the theoretical and practical advantage of PIAGET's theory if IQ-measured intelligence is thereby proven to be similar in character to scholastic achievement tests; such similarity would be undesirable for an evaluation of operative intelligence. I close this paragraph on scholastic validity by reminding the reader of the origin of intelligence tests: BINET devised his tests as an instrument of selection of retarded children for public education. Are schools meant to select and adapt children to the school, or should the school adapt itself to the psychological development of the child? If the teaching profession and society at large is ready to choose the second alternative, PIAGET's theory may turn out to be of immense practical utility [FURTH, 1970].

The assumption of a relatively homogeneous environment is implicit in the concept of any standard measure that claims to represent a person's potential as distinct from his achievement. The ideal of a culture-free intelligence test keeps constantly coming up and represents the counterpart of this homogeneous environment idea. In this respect the IQ test tradition finds itself in a curious situation. In the early part of its history the hereditary character of IQ was almost universally accepted. Consequently the fact of differing environments did not create any serious problems. But with the gradual emergence of an associationistic stimulus-response model in which every human behavior was said to be explainable in terms of similar learning processes due to environmental stimuli, the difference between intelligence and learned achievement became theoretically indefensible. Investigators discovered with surprise the modifiability of IQ [e.g., SKEELS, 1966]. Naturally, what is learned can be forgotten or, if greater incentives are provided, can be learned better. To bolster an impossible theoretical posture one must have recourse to a presumed standard environment. In fact in studies where mean IQ differences are used to claim the intellectual superiority or inferiority of certain groups of people, control of environmental conditions is now a routinely accepted methodological precaution.

However, on what grounds can one assume that environmental factors – whatever their nature – are normally distributed? Do parental love and acceptance, emotional and economic stability of the family, to mention just some universally recognized important factors, come along a continuum that fits the standard curve? If one begins to question the quantitative continuity and considers that a certain quantitative diminution brings about easily recognizable qualitative changes (e.g., poverty, parental neglect), the whole statistical interpretation of environmental comparability and of interactive factors becomes suspect. In short, the theory underlying the measurement of IQ makes presumptions about the environment that are not confirmed by empirical evidence.

Interestingly, PIAGET's biological theory does have a solid basis for the common human aspect of the environment; this is the counterpart of the common operative aspect of development which all human beings share. But it was shown above that these aspects have no separate existence from individual contingencies. The common human environment may adequately explain the common human aspects of intellectual development, but it cannot become the basis for a normally distributed range of individual performances.

This leads to the last point relative to IQ measures, namely the assumption that performance provides reasonable evidence for intelligence. PIAGET and his associates have consistently rejected this assumption. Their position follows logically from the conceptual distinction between a particular overt performance and the underlying mechanism or operative capacity. As I<small>NHELDER</small> [1966] puts it: 'To determine that a subject is capable of solving such and such a problem is one thing, while to understand *how* he manages to do so is quite another' (p. 300). I<small>NHELDER</small> has been the person in Geneva most closely associated with what can be called a Piagetian equivalent of an IQ test, ever since she published in 1943 a first application of P<small>IAGET'S</small> tasks to the diagnosis of mental retardation [I<small>NHELDER</small>, 1968].

I<small>NHELDER'S</small> observations highlight in a profound manner the difference between the IQ approach and the operative assessment. Whereas the IQ approach uses more or less arbitrary cut-off points at 75 or at 50 and is open to administrative and social abuses of which we now are only too painfully aware, I<small>NHELDER</small> interprets the character of the retarded intelligence in terms of P<small>IAGET'S</small> theory as follows. Mildly retarded persons are those whose thinking remains closed at the concrete stage; they show no indication of being open toward the formal stage. Severely retarded persons are those who do not reach the stage of concrete operations. Briefly, I<small>NHELDER'S</small> diagnosis is based on an operative assessment by means of a clinical interview; it includes a qualitative explanation of retardation motivated in terms of its own theory. In distinction, the quantitative indicant of an age-dependent intelligence quotient by itself reveals nothing about the character of the thinking deficiency.

Significantly, this early success in describing mental retardation within P<small>IAGET'S</small> framework has not been matched by a comparable success in substituting his operative tasks for the more common uses of IQ tests. For over 20 years attempts at meaningful standardization of P<small>IAGET'S</small> tasks have been undertaken, notably in Geneva, in North America and in other parts of the world. Both from a theoretical and empirical angle I am suprised that Genevans regard with equanimity recurrent efforts to construct what is sometimes called a superior type of IQ test. This test would be based on standardized age norms for the acquisition of certain Piagetian tasks and stages. Perhaps this is partly due to P<small>IAGET'S</small> disinclination to make any firm statements about the adequacy or inadequacy of how his theory is being interpreted and applied. He does not consider himself the founder of a 'school' that has to monitor its followers.

But it is surely instructive to note the difference between the meaning of the word intelligence when applied to the description of developmental stages or to the diagnosis of certain deficiencies and the different meaning when applied to interindividual differences. For the first purpose PIAGET'S theory is eminently applicable and has produced potentially exciting results in investigation of retarded, aphasic, psychotic and senile persons. The theory has also shown its fruitfulness in describing the intellectual development of persons deprived of usual channels of experience, namely, blind and deaf children. For the second purpose of differential psychology PIAGET'S theory itself seems to indicate, as I attempted to demonstrate in earlier sections, that individual differences cannot fall under a general norm. When one encounters significant time lags in performance, PIAGET thinks, one can explain them, but only after the event: 'It is not possible to have a general theory of these resistances' [GREEN *et al.*, 1971, p. 11].

PIAGET'S principal contribution is his elaboration of the mechanisms of knowledge; these mechanisms are the basis of any intelligent performance and any specific learning. To attempt to measure the amount of this common intelligence is like measuring life or health. When something is substantially wrong with one's physical health, medical experts can probably diagnose a deficiency or a disfunction. But the vast bulk of the population could not possibly be placed along a cumulative continuum. Society is quite satisfied if the medical practitioner after a thorough check-up pronounces a patient in good health. If nothing more exact suffices with physiologic mechanisms which are precise in functioning and much more readily observable why should one expect a greater exactness with psychological mechanisms that function in order to open the human organism to the limitless inventions of the human spirit? During a 1969 conference on measurement and Piagetian theory, PIAGET insisted that the main problem of development is to establish the method of construction of true novelties. The novelties invented by the individual, PIAGET says [GREEN *et al.*, 1971, p. 212], 'do not stem simply from the potentialities of the human race as a whole – we cannot yet even imagine to what heights human invention will lead –', but they also come about through individual initiative and individual or interindividual activities.

It is, therefore, a mistake to assume that performance even on PIAGET'S tasks can be taken as a direct reflection of specific stage dependent thinking mechanisms. This implies among other things that operative tasks have to be adapted to different sociocultural contexts. These settings have a powerful influence not merely on the particular content to which operative mechanisms are applied but also on the manner in which these mechanisms are used. PIAGET'S associate BOVET [1970] reported that Algerian children seemed at first strikingly successful in conservation of matter in contrast to conservation of length. Additional probes made clear that this was an unstable pseudoconservation. Such apparent discrepancies from Western performance patterns were interpreted as due to differing day-to-day activities and cultural experiences.

To conclude this section on IQ tests I would interpret PIAGET's position as incompatible with any individual score that purports to show the innate potential, the general learning ability or whatever other descriptions are used to distinguish IQ from achievement measures. There remains the final question as to how PIAGET envisages the relation of what he calls intelligence to heredity.

Intelligence and Heredity

For PIAGET, intelligence is not a content but a mechanism of individual construction; we can, therefore, understand that he is not merely opposed to a consideration of intelligence as caused by mechanisms of learning of environmental information. He is likewise opposed to the view that attributes the source of intelligence to hereditary transmission of genetic information: 'If, biologically speaking, learning and heredity and its content are excluded, there remains this fundamental reality... which constitutes the necessary preliminary condition for every kind of learning and even for heredity itself: namely, the organizing function with its absolute continuity a function which is not transmitted but is continuous, conserving itself from transmission to transmission' [PIAGET, 1971, p. 322]. Anatomical features, physiological functioning and certain forms of instinctual behavior can be said to be tied to structures transmitted by heredity. But the extraordinary constructive plasticity and the generality and eventual necessity of human intelligence cannot in PIAGET's theory derive merely from organically-tied hereditary structures. When PIAGET proposes that the structures of intelligence have their source in the genetically evolving and individually developing knowledge that reflects on its own equilibrated functioning, the question whether heredity or learning is more important in human intelligence loses all its meaning. In this sense PIAGET's biological theory is both revolutionary and liberating. One can only hope that its widespread popularity today is not merely a reaction to the abuses to which the IQ tradition has led – of which the nature-nurture controversy is a prime example – but that PIAGET's theory can become the occasion for a more humanly relevant, that is, biologically grounded, perspective on intelligence and the human person.

References

Bovet, M.: Piaget's theory of cognitive development, sociocultural difference, and mental retardation; in Haywood Social-cultural aspects of mental retardation (Appleton-Century-Crofts, New York 1970).

Furth, H.G.: Piaget for teachers (Prentice-Hall, Englewood Cliffs, N.J. 1970).

Green, D.R.; Ford, M.P., and Flamer, G.B.: Measurement and Piaget (McGraw-Hill, New York 1971).

Inhelder, B.: Cognitive development and its contribution to the diagnosis of some phenomena of mental deficiency. Merrill-Palmer Quart. Behav. Develop. *12:* 299–319 (1966).

Inhelder, B.: The diagnosis of reasoning in the mentally retarded (original 1943) (John Day, New York 1968).

Inhelder, B.: Developmental theory and diagnostic procedures; in Green, Ford and Flamer Measurement and Piaget. (McGraw-Hill, New York 1971).

Inhelder, B. and Piaget, J.: The early growth of logic in the child (original 1959) (Norton, New York 1969).

Piaget, J.: The child's conception of the world (original 1926) (Littlefield, Adams & Co., Totowa, N.J. 1969).

Piaget, J.: Science of education and the psychology of the child (original 1969) (Orion, New York 1970).

Piaget, J.: Biology and knowledge (original 1967) (University of Chicago Press, Chicago 1971).

Piaget, J.: Intellectual evolution from adolescence to adulthood (original, 1970). Human Develop. *15:* 1–12 (1972).

Piaget, J. and Inhelder, B.: Mental imagery in the child (original 1966) (Basic Books, New York 1971).

Skeels, H.M.: Adult status of children with contrasting early life experience. Monogr. Soc. Res. Child Dev. *31:* No. 3 (serial No. 105) (1966).

Request reprints from: Dr. H.G. Furth, Department of Psychology, Catholic University of America, *Washington, DC 20017* (USA)

Human Develop. *16:* 74–89 (1973)

On the Assumptive Base of the Nature-Nurture Controversy: Additive versus Interactive Conceptions

W. F. OVERTON

Temple University, Philadelphia, Pa.

Abstract. This essay inquires into the major conceptual features of the nature-nurture issue and explores theoretical, methodological, and empirical dimensions which derive from the conceptual. It is maintained that the most basic issues are reflections of a paradigm clash between opposing world views. At the pretheoretical level the clash is represented by one perspective which asserts nature-nurture to be additive and another which asserts they are interactive. Both within paradigm and between paradigm differences are discussed.

Key Words
Nature
Nurture
Scientific paradigm
Mechanistic world view
Organismic world view
Additive paradigm
Interactive paradigm

Frequently derided as an outdated and sterile debate, and as often acclaimed as an important problem; frequently proclaimed to be a dead issue and as often resurrected as a lively area of inquiry; frequently the target of methodological and conceptual criticisms, and as frequently the source of new methods and sophisticated data, the 'nature-nurture' or 'heredity-environment' issue continues to run its cyclical course. It is doubtful whether, for better or worse, any issue has had a longer ranging or more ubiquitous role in the development of psychology than has this one. Beginning in philosophy, the question involved whether certain basic types of knowledge were innately given in man or whether all knowledge and the means for attaining knowledge was acquired though sensory experience. In that sphere the problem – often termed the 'nativist-empiricist issue' – has been and continues to be closely tied to idealist and rationalist philosophical positions on the one hand, and realist and empiricist positions on the other. With the advent of psychology proper, the major issue came to concern the specific contributions of hereditary structures (along with the maturational unfolding of these structures) and environmental factors to the origin and development of behavior. In this field it has come to permeate virtually every area of interest from animal behavior (innate or acquired?) to human action, language, perception, motivation, personality, and intelligence.

Nature-Nurture

The Questions

It is both impressive and significant that despite its long history and pervasiveness, the general form of the issue has changed very little. Although, as suggested by ANASTASI [1958], the question of 'Which' factor, heredity or environment, determines behavior and development was superseded by the question of 'How much' each factor contributes, this change is, upon analysis, more apparent than real. Even those who maintained the most extreme positions and ascribed causation to one or the other factor, e.g., WATSON and GESELL, did not assert the total absence of the other component [WHITE, 1968]. Rather, they maintained that for analytic purposes one or the other could effectively be ignored and designated as having a zero value [SPIKER, 1966]. The emergence of the question 'How much' was conditioned by the establishment of quantitative methods which permitted more precise estimates of the proportional contribution of each factor. Thus, the zero value of the 'Which' question became the 10- or 20-percent value of the 'How much' question.

A second change in the form of the nature-nurture issue which was also suggested by ANASTASI [1958], was from the question 'How much' to the question 'How'. Although the problem of how specific hereditary and specific environmental factors influence various characteristics is distinguishably different from the question 'How much' it will be argued later that rather than being a *change* in the form of the issue, the question 'How' represents an independent alternative to the 'How much' question and one that has been contesting it throughout history.

The duration, pervasiveness, cyclical nature, and lack of any meaningful change in the form of the questions asked suggests that at very least the nature-nurture issue involves more than mere empirical or factual problems. Certainly, if the problems were merely empirical someone or some group of the many investigators who have explored the issue would have by this time provided us with a satisfactory form of solution. This not being the case, it is necessary to look elsewhere for solutions or at least resolutions. It is the thesis of this essay that while there are important empirical matters relevant to the nature-nurture controversy, these are secondary to and derived from deep-rooted conceptual features. In the following pages these conceptual features will be explored and the implication of these features for empirical inquiry will be discussed.

Conceptual Issues

Earlier Views

To assert the nature-nurture issue entails conceptual factors is not in itself unique. A number of investigators have accepted this point and have presented conceptual re-analyses of the issue [see for example, ANASTASI, 1958; ANASTASI and FOLEY, 1948; CARMICHAEL, 1925; HIRSCH, 1970; LEHRMAN, 1970; LOEVINGER, 1943]. However, many such analyses have often shared a number of positions which are at variance with the present viewpoint. The first of these has been the idea that the conceptual differences entailed in the issue are relatively superficial in nature and hence open to definitional or semantic solutions. This view has resulted in what might be termed the 'reasonable men principle', i.e., the notion that if men would simply be reasonable and agree to certain definitions, the nature-nurture controversy would dissolve and science could get on with its 'rightful' empirical tasks. Thus, for example, if men would merely agree that it is possible or, on the other hand, that it is impossible to categorize various behaviors, traits, or characteristics as innate or learned, the controversy would be ended. While there is a certain reality to this view it fails to recognize that such agreement would be analogous to maintaining that historically, reasonable men should have simply agreed that the sun rather than the earth is the center of the universe, or that material objects be understood as static rather than active, or light be accepted as particles rather than waves. The point here is that agreement on definitions concerning the nature-nurture issue involves commitments to principles which are at least as deep-rooted as these past paradigm disputes. In fact, a probable reason for the very endurance of the nature-nurture issue *qua* issue lies in the failure of psychology to recognize it as being based on a paradigm dispute and continuing to view it as a simple empirical matter perhaps vulgarized by conceptual features.

A second position frequently exhibited by those presenting various conceptual re-analyses is closely related to the reasonable men principle. Not only has it been maintained that solutions rest on superficial conceptual definitions but frequently this assertion further entails a specification as to which particular definitions are correct. Thus, there is both an appeal to reasonable men and a description of the identity of the reasonable men. This absolutistic attitude is usually manifested in statements implying or openly stating that the other party is 'conceptually confused', 'missed the point', 'takes a defeatist attitude', etc. It is apparent that this attitude is also a reflection of a denial of the possibility of alternative paradigms of explanation. Its effect is polemic and relegates counter-arguments to the realm of error. The presence of contradictions is abhorrent within this view and apparent contradictory positions are explained away as mere appearances.

A final feature often shared by those who have explored conceptual dimensions of the nature-nurture issue, and one which is also closely related to the others, is the imposition of a strict historical continuity on the problem. As with contemporary contradictions, historical events are interpreted as totally linear, additive processes despite available contradictory evidence. An example of this is the suggestion that the issue of the relative influence of hereditary and environmental factors (the question, 'How much') led directly, through the elaboration of the analysis-of-variance model, to questions concerning the interaction between heredity and environment ('How') [ANANDALAKSHMY and GRINDER, 1970]. This interpretation occurs despite the fact that at least as early as 1925, CARMICHAEL was maintaining a strong interactionist position in his assertion that there is, 'a real and inviolable *interdependence* between maturation and learning. From the moment that growth has begun... development consists in the alteration of existing structures and functions. Such modification, however, can only occur by the interaction of the hereditary-environmentally produced individual and an ever changing environment' [CARMICHAEL, 1925, p. 260]. The additive interpretation of history represents a confusion between the temporal and logical order of events wherein the temporal succession of calendar time is applied to ideas which might better be viewed as synchronic. The motivation of this interpretation derives from the same source as the other positions described above; an attempt to deny the reality of competing paradigms.

An Alternative Paradigm View

I would suggest that a more productive approach concerning the conceptual dimensions of the nature-nurture issue is one which abandons each of these earlier versions – the reasonable men principle, the absolutistic attitude toward truth and error, and the interpretation of history as a strict continuity of ideas – and substitutes in their place a reinterpretation of history which recognizes that contradictory conceptions having equal validity may co-exist and develop individually over extended periods of time. This proposal, when applied to the nature-nurture issue, asserts that there have been two *truly alternative conceptions* of the problem. On the one hand, there is a conception which most basically asserts that any behavior, trait, or characteristic can be analyzed into individual components representing genetic factors and environment factors. Empirical work within this tradition has generally examined which factors or how much each factor contributes to a particular phenomenon. The historical change from the question 'Which' to the question 'How much' represented a development *within* this tradition analogous to the movement from a hard to a soft or statistical determinism in the physical sciences.

On the other hand, there is the conception that most behaviors, traits, and characteristics are the result of *strong interactions* between genetic and environmental features and over the course of development it becomes impossible to distinguish in any meaningful way individual components. Empirical work in this tradition has tended to examine how specific genetic or environmental features affect the normal developmental course of the phenomenon in question. It should be recognized that this is a very different approach from that of breaking the phenomenon itself into components. Thus, as mentioned earlier, the question 'How' is seen not as an outgrowth of earlier questions but as a viable alternative to such questions.

Before specifying some implications of this alternative viewpoint as well as presenting some details of each alternative, it is important to be explicit concerning the status of the alternatives themselves. They are not proposed as empirical generalizations or even theoretical statements, at least not in the narrow sense of that term. Rather they have a pretheoretical character in that they represent metatheoretical presuppositions basic to the construction of any theory. In a series of papers, written with my colleague, HAYNE REESE [OVERTON and REESE, 1972; REESE and OVERTON, 1970], we examined the nature and details of such presuppositions, pretheoretic models, or paradigms. The significant fact is that they point in two directions. On the one hand, these models are themselves formulated within the context of general metaphysical world views and epistemological models. On the other hand, they provide the determining context for the formulation of more concrete models and thus ultimately determine the types of questions that will and will not be asked and the type of methodologies that will and will not be employed. There are levels of models then, and while models formulated at any one level are partially independent of models at other levels, there is a categorical determinism which extends across levels. Because world views differ in such basic categories as truth criteria and the nature of substance and change, models and other conceptions based on different world views are incompatible and irreconcilable [KUHN, 1970; OVERTON and REESE, 1972; PEPPER, 1942]. They function as alternative representations of phenomena and although they provide prescriptions for theory formations and empirical work, they are not themselves open to empirical determination. They closely resemble sets of rules and as such they are never true or false, but rather, more or less adequate in guiding our conduct.

I am suggesting that the alternative conceptions of nature-nurture as (a) decomposable into additive components versus (b) non-decomposable due to strong interactions across the course of development, are truly alternatives precisely because they are pretheoretical and are constructed within the context of incompatible world views. Specifically, it seems that, and this will be more fully elaborated later, the former alternative is a reflection of a mechanistic world view whereas the latter reflects an organismic world view.

Implications

This interpretation of the nature-nurture issue as a problem that emerges from a basic paradigm clash has a number of implications. First and foremost, it means that the conceptual dimensions of the dispute are large indeed and any immediate 'resolution' entails recognition of the incompatible, irreconcilable and non-empirical character of the alternative views, i.e. a kind of agreement to disagree. Ultimately, one or the other of the alternatives, or some third position, may triumph but like the story of the old soldier it is doubtful that the loser will die in the battle of an empirical clash; more likely it will fade away from neglect and disuse.

A second implication of the alternative conceptions viewpoint is that the nature-nurture issue is really a multi-leveled problem involving different issues and different methods of approach to the issues at each level. At the most general level, i.e., *between* pretheoretical paradigms, the issues concern choices of our image of the nature of the universe, man, and knowledge. Here the approach taken is principally rational and entails only dim traces of the empirical. At a less general level, but *within* a particular paradigm, more specific theoretical conceptions are formulated. Thus, within the additive paradigm, theoretical conceptions have been proposed which have stressed the innate [LORENZ, 1965], or maturational [GESELL, 1954], the learned [HULL, 1943; SKINNER, 1971], or the proportional contribution of each of these factors [e.g., BURT, 1972; CATTELL, 1970; JENSEN, 1969; NICHOLS, 1965; VANDENBERG, 1962]. Within the interactional paradigm, the resultant theoretical conceptions have emphasized the interactional character of the developmental process [e.g., PIAGET, 1971; HUNT, 1961; KOHLBERG, 1968; LEHRMAN, 1970]. The theories in turn ultimately lead to methodological and empirical issues which are, of course, then directly open to various research approaches.

The Within Paradigm Debate

In order to elaborate on implications of the alternative conceptions viewpoint, we may focus on some of the recent literature covering the concept of 'heritability' as this has been applied to intelligence and the understanding of differences in IQ scores between ethnic or racial groups [JENSEN, 1969]. Heritability (h^2), 'refers to the proportion of population *variance* in some particular characteristic (e.g. IQ) attributable to genetic factors ($1-h^2$ is, therefore, the proportion of variance attributable to nongenetic factors, that is, environment and measurement error)' [JENSEN, 1971, p. 394]. Empirical findings relevant to this concept (i.e., data on IQ scores for individuals of different kinships including monozygotic and dizygotic twins and various rearing conditions) have generally led to heritability estimates of approximately 80%, thus leaving around 20% to be accounted for by error and environmental influences. From this base the argument has been made by JENSEN [1969] that lower mean IQ scores for Negros can largely be accounted for by genetic factors.

The concept of heritability is quite clearly based within an additive paradigm. From the very statistical model it employs, i.e., the components of variance model, to the theory of knowledge it assumes, i.e., the analytic ideal, the constant image thrust forth is one in which every event – whether a particular test score or some general characteristic of nature – is understood as being a *linear function of independent elements*. Furthermore, it does not change the situation any to maintain that this position does consider interactions by introducing an interaction term into the analysis of variance [JENSEN, 1969, p. 39]. As discussed by OVERTON and REESE [1972], such interaction effects, 'are themselves linear, since they are defined as population cell means minus the sum of main effects (plus the population base rate)' (p. 84). In fact, the very use of the term 'interaction' within this paradigm indicates that definitions of terms are not model independent (see OVERTON and REESE [1972], for an elaboration of different model related uses of the term 'interaction').

What then are some of the criticisms that have been raised concerning the concept of heritability? Within paradigm criticisms, from the empirical through the theoretical, will first be discussed and these will be followed by between paradigm criticisms. A recent discussion by KAMIN [1972] in which he asserted that a good deal of the twin intelligence score data are simply fallacious, illustrates the most obvious empirical criticism. SCARR-SALAPATEK'S [1971] work on the measurement of different heritability estimates between different social class groups, an investigation which had not been conducted prior to JENSEN's [1969] article, is also an empirically directed criticism. The significant point is that in both cases – and this is the theme that runs through all *within* paradigm criticisms – acceptance of the critique does nothing to alter the basic form of the argument. Acceptance merely entails quantitative changes in the heritability estimate, perhaps to a ratio favoring the environmental rather than the genetic component. In any event, it does not argue against the concept of heritability itself.

At a more general methodological level, LIGHT and SMITH [1969], using a simulation technique, employed JENSEN's own additive statistical model, his estimates of the parameters of the genetic component (0.75), the environmental component (0.24) and the statistical interaction (0.01) and, 'demonstrated that it is possible to account for the entire 15 point [IQ] gap [between blacks and whites] without resort to the hypothesis of genetic differences between average intellectual capacities of blacks and whites' [LIGHT and SMITH, 1971, p. 352]. (For a continuing exchange on the pros and cons of this methodological reinterpretation see also SHOCKLEY [1971 a, b].) Other methodologicial criticisms include arguments that: (a) the assumption of random mating essential to the mathematical model of heritability does not hold [HIRSCH, 1967 a, b] and the counter argument that assortative mating would most probably be positive (i.e. high IQ individuals mating with other high IQ individuals) and hence lead to a conservative estimate of heritability [BRELAND, 1972]; (b) there is a confounding of hereditary and environmental influences in twin studies [FEHR, 1969]; (c) the representativeness of studies of twins and sibling reared apart is questionable [CROW, 1969, KAMIN, 1972]; (d) heritability values are limited to specific populations [HIRSCH, 1970].

As with empirical criticisms, within paradigm methodological criticisms again involve no suggestion for a change in the form of the argument. This same situation is further demonstrated at the final within paradigm level, i.e. the theoretical. For example, BEREITER [1969, 1970] despite the fact that he maintains a very environmentally oriented theoretical attitude, does not even argue directly against the 80% genetic – 20% environment ratio of the heritability estimate. Instead, his primary focus is directed toward the point that within the limits imposed by genetic factors there is ample room for the exercise of environmental determinants.

Before turning directly to *between* paradigm criticism of heritability, it should be noted that some critiques do not lend themselves to immediate classification into one or the other of the paradigm categories. A case in point is the criticism of the use of intelligence tests in the assessment of intelligence [e.g., ELKIND, 1969; KAGAN, 1972; LIGHT, 1972; McCLELLAND, 1973]. To the extent such criticisms maintain that the tests employed are not reliable indicators of competence or are not culture free or culture fair, etc. it seems that these, too, are arguments within the additive paradigm. That is, from this perspective a change in the tests employed would result in a different heritability estimate, not a repudiation of heritability itself. On the other hand, to the degree that the argument opposes psychometric conceptions of intelligence and substitutes in their place alternative understandings of the very nature of intelligence, then the critique is based on an alternative viewpoint and hence, represents a between paradigm criticism.

The Between Paradigm Dispute

The legitimate work of criticism between paradigms consists of offering an alternative viewpoint which is an adequate representation of the phenomena and which is discontinuous in the sense of being incompatible with the other position. Adequacy of representation is a historical judgment and the alternatives vie with each other for the attention of the scientific community through the course of history. The process continues along two tracks. On the one hand, each perspective attempts to document its adequacy by demonstrating the fruitfulness of the type of questions it raises and the answers it provides. On the other hand, each attempts to demonstrate the weakness of some central assumptions of the other. It is only when these points are not recognized that the reasonable men principle, absolutistic attitudes, and continuity of ideas substitute for a true paradigm clash.

If the paradigm of nature-nurture that ultimately yields the heritability estimate is one which asserts events are decomposable into additive components, its alternative is the interactive paradigm. This maintains that many events are the result of strong interactions occurring across the course of development and as a consequence, they are not decomposable into individual components. An early theoretical statement of this position was made by CARMICHAEL: 'The fact as it appears to the present writer is that no distinction can be expediently made at any given moment in the behavior of the individual, after the fertilized egg has once begun to develop, between that which is native and that which is acquired. The so-called hereditary factors can only be acquired in response to an environment and likewise the so-called acquired factors can only be secured by a modification of already existing structure, which in the last analysis is hereditary structure' [1925, p. 257].

Here, there is a distinct alternative to the concept of heritability in that acceptance of this view, by definition, results in the rejection of the calculation of estimates of proportional contributions of nature and nurture. Piaget's theory asserts an identical position in its conceptualization of development as an ongoing series of actions which incorporate environmental events into (initially hereditary) structures and result in qualitative transformations in the structure due to the incorporation [PIAGET and INHELDER, 1969]. HUNT [1969] advances a similar theoretical view through the proposal that intelligence is, 'a cumulative, dynamic product of the ongoing informational and intentional interaction of infants and young children with their physical and social circumstances' (p. 284). In turn, HUNT [1969] employs this concept as an interpretative framework for discussing evidence pertaining to the role of environment and the role of heredity in development.

Approaching the problem from a more genetically oriented position than the foregoing theorists, HIRSCH [1970], nevertheless, arrives at the same alternative conception. His statement that, 'the plain facts are that in the study of man a heritability estimate turns out to be a piece of "knowledge" that is both deceptive and trivial' [HIRSCH, 1970, p. 98] is at least partially based on his rejection of additive assumptions and his acceptance of genotypes – environment interactions reflected in the 'norm-of-reaction' concept (i.e. for different environmental conditions the same genotype can produce different phenotypes) [HIRSCH, 1967a, b]. The work of individuals such as WEISS [1971] and WADDINGTON [1971] in the field of theoretical biology, illustrates similar views, e.g. 'between the genotype space and the phenotype space... there is a whole series of processes in which various genetic instructions *interact* with one another and *interact* also with the conditions of the environment in which the organism is developing' [WADDINGTON, 1971, p. 364, emphasis added].

Although he makes no direct reference to the nature-nurture issue, WOHLWILL'S [1970] consideration of the age variable in psychological research represents an important methodological contribution to the interactive conception. One aspect of WOHLWILL'S [1970] proposal is that the *general course of development* for certain variables should be treated as normative. These developmental variables are those 'for which the general course of development (considered in terms of direction, form, sequence, etc.) remains invariant over a broad range of particular environmental conditions... as well as genetic characteristics' [WOHLWILL, 1970, p. 52]. In essence, this is an acceptance of the idea of strong interactions occurring across development and a suggestion that as a consequence, the variables (e.g. intelligence) so affected be viewed as outside the realm of characteristics decomposable into genetic and environmental components.

A final step in the argument is that specific environmental conditions or specific genetic conditions may affect the rate and terminal level of the characteristics which are not themselves decomposable. This in turn is exactly the question, 'How' suggested by ANASTASI [1958]. That is, for example, it may be asserted that intelligence is not itself decomposable into genetic and environmental factors while at the same time, maintaining through empirical investigation, that being raised in a deprived or enriched environment or having a specific genetic deficit may affect the rate of development and terminal level of intelligence. TANNER [1970] explores similar considerations in relationship to physical growth.

We have here, then the paradigm clash. Negatively considered, each side disputes the legitimacy of the primary assumption of the other and repudiates the meaningfulness of its approach. Positively, each view leads to its own theories, methods, interpretations, and empirical inquiry. It is not, however, at the empirical level that the issue between the paradigms can be decided, for there is no such thing as a crucial test among divergent assumptions. In fact, in an effort to establish its adequacy, each side interprets various empirical work within its own categories. A case in point is HUNT's use of the SKEELS and DYE [1939] study of the effect of a restricted environment on IQ scores along with the follow-up study some years later [SKEELS, 1966] as support for his interaction argument. BEREITER [1970], however, argues that this evidence is just as adequately accounted for by a model which maintains a heritability ratio of 80%. An alternative conceptions view would maintain that although the empirical studies entailed are themselves significant, they are not the material upon which to make decisions concerning a paradigm dispute.

Additive and Interactive Conceptions

The Assumptive Base

It was suggested earlier that the pretheoretical paradigms point in two directions. Thus far, the discussion has focused upon the effect of the paradigms on theory construction, methodology, and empirical observation. In order to elaborate on how deep-rooted, conceptual, and incompatible these paradigms are we may turn to explore their determination in the context of general world views. The extent and manner in which world views, especially the mechanistic and organismic world views, have shaped our scientific paradigms in psychology has been detailed elsewhere [OVERTON and REESE, 1972; REESE and OVERTON, 1970]. Here, the effect may be briefly sketched by noting two perspectives concerning the nature of substance. On the one hand, it was considered to be one of NEWTON's great accomplishments that he viewed matter as basically static [PROSCH, 1964]. On the other hand, EINSTEIN is proported to have maintained that matter is simply energy slowed down, i.e. activity is basic.

The acceptance of substance as static led to the Newtonian mechanical world view represented by the billiard ball metaphor, i.e., 'basically everything... was made up of small solid particles, in themselves always inert, but always in motion and elastically rebounding from each other... and operating mechanically' [PROSCH, 1964, p. 66]. Within this perspective, if one inquires as to how a complex event is to be understood, the answer is that, like the understanding of a simple machine, the event is to be decomposed (analyzed) into even more and more simple parts until the ultimate static substance or reality is found. The simple components are then interrelated in unidirectional and linear causal sequence according to the *law of identity*. This analytic ideal of course entails the additivity of parts. It is the world view that ultimately results in the view of nature and nurture as decomposable into individual 'real' components. Given the pervasive character of the analytic ideal, there is little wonder that even in the face of doubts at different levels, the 'hope' of additivity is maintained. A number of authors have expressed concern that at the genetic level gene actions may be epistatic rather than additive [BRELAND, 1972; CROW, 1969; DOBZHANSKY, 1972], and others have questioned the additivity assumption of the components of variance model [HIRSCH, 1967; HUNT, 1961; LOEVINGER, 1943]. If the matter were merely an empirical hypothesis, perhaps these doubts would be sufficient to give up the idea of additivity. Such, however, is not the case with world views.

If activity rather than static properties is taken as primary, a different world view and different scientific paradigms emerge. If events are constantly changing and coming into being through their activity, then the first step in understanding is the discovery – in the rational sense – of a system or organization within which this change occurs. This critical feature of the process of understanding within the organismic world view has been articulated in many different ways depending on the specific purpose. It is the establishment of a sufficient reason for an event or a sufficient cause; it is the discovery of being in becoming, constancy in change; when viewed as diachronic it is the postulation of a developmental path (a final cause or *telos*); when seen as synchronic it is the basis of a structuralism (formal cause).

The discovery of a system or organization for an event does not terminate the process of understanding but it does provide the major conceptual features, or the conceptual context, within which further understanding may proceed. Again returning to the idea of activity, the action of subsystems within the total event cannot be analyzed in terms of one-way causality. Since both or all subsystems are themselves active there is reciprocal causality, a dialectic [RATNER, 1971] or an interaction [VON BERTALANFFY, 1968] between them. This means that there are no completely independent efficient causes (independent variables or forces acting upon dependent variables), or as BUNGE [1963] expressed it: 'Efficient causes are effective solely to the extent to which they trigger, enhance, or damp inner processes... [p. 195]. An adequate picture is provided by a synthesis of self-determination [organismic activity] and extrinsic determination [environmental activity]... The two exaggerations of environmentalism and innatism... are thereby avoided [p. 197].'

If the positon described here, however, were taken to its logical extreme it would in fact preclude empirical inquiry for there would be no way to attribute any role to individual components. In the investigation of nature-nurture, for example, the interactions between components would preclude identification of the components themselves. To avoid this position, a distinction is maintained between strong and weak interactions. In the nature-nurture problem, the continual reciprocity between genetic and environmental activity occurring before conception, through to the time of testing for intelligence would constitute a strong interaction, not decomposable. Relatively short-term occurrences, well defined features, and traumatic events, on the other hand might be analyzed under the convenient fiction that they are independent, i.e. weak interactions. To the extent this fiction is considered reasonable, the traditional experimental procedures and statistical techniques are appropriate. At the point that strong interactions appear, these traditional analytic procedures break down and different types of questions are asked [OVERTON and REESE, 1972].

PIAGET'S [PIAGET and INHELDER, 1969] concept of intelligence is the most articulate theoretical specification of the organismic understanding, and also its most consistent application to the nature-nurture problem. Although the theory and its implications are discussed elsewhere in this symposium some of its major features may be used as illustrative. Starting from a conception of intelligence as activity, PIAGET first postulates the diachronic organization. This is the equilibration model which maintains that the activity of intelligence is directed toward the *telos* of the highest state of equilibrium possible. Next, within this developmental dimension, PIAGET describes the structures of the activity – sensorimotor, concrete and formal operational structures. Further specification is provided by the recognition that the structures are moments in the expression of strong interactions or a reciprocity between what the organism initially provided (nature) and that provided by the environment (nurture). Thus, the intelligence of sensorimotor structures or of operational structures cannot be decomposed into individual components. However, it is most reasonable to inquire *How* specific environmental activity or specific genetic activity (weak interactions) affect the rate or terminal level of intelligence.

In conclusion, these then are the most basic conceptual dimensions of the nature-nurture issue, i.e. opposing world views. Each leads to its own scientific paradigms, theories, methods and empirical inquiries, and each entails significant issues at every level. Furthermore, each perspective is incompatible with the other and the choice between them appears to be more of a rational than empirical activity.

References

ANANDALAKSHMY, S. and GRINDER, R.E.: Conceptual emphasis in the history of developmental psychology. Evolutionary theory, teleology, and the nature-nurture issue. Child Develop. *41:* 1113–1123 (1970).

ANASTASI, A.: Heredity, environment, and the question 'How?' Psychol. Rev. *65:* 197–208 (1958).

ANASTASI, A. and FOLEY, J.P.: A proposed reorientation in the heredity-environment controversy. Psychol. Rev. *55:* 239–249 (1948).

BEREITER, C.: The future of individual differences. Harv. educ. Rev. *39:* 310–318 (1969).

BEREITER, C.: Genetics and educability. Educational implications of the Jensen debate; in HELLMUTH Disadvantaged child, vol. 3, pp. 279–299 (Bruner/Mazel, New York 1970).

BERTALANFFY, L. VON: General system theory (Braziller, New York 1968).

BRELAND, N.S.: Heredity and environmental sources of trait variation and co-variation; unpubl. Ph.D. diss. Buffalo (1972).

BUNGE, M.: Causality. The place of the causal principle in modern science (World Publishing, New York 1963).

BURT, C.: Inheritance of general intelligence. Amer. Psychol. 27: 175–190 (1972).

CARMICHAEL, L.: Heredity and environment. Are they antithetical. J. abnorm. soc. Psychol. 20: 245–260 (1925).

CATTELL, R.B.: Separating endogenous, exogenous, ecogenic, and epogenic component curves in developmental data. Develop. Psychol. 3: 151–162 (1970).

CROW, J.: Genetic theories and influences. Comments on the value of diversity. Harv. educ. Rev. 39: 301–309 (1969).

DOBZHANSKY, T.: Genetics and the diversity of behavior. Amer. Psychol. 27: 523–530 (1972).

ELKIND, D.: Piagetian and psychometric conceptions of intelligence. Harv. educ. Rev. 39: 319–337 (1969).

FEHR, F.S.: Critique of hereditarian accounts of 'intelligence' and contrary findings. Harv. educ. Rev. 39: 571–580 (1969).

GESELL, A.: The ontogenesis of infant behavior; in CARMICHAEL Manual of child psychology, pp. 335–373 (Wiley, New York 1954).

HIRSCH, J.: Behavior-genetic analysis (McGraw-Hill, New York 1967a).

HIRSCH, J.: Behavior-genetic or 'experimental' analysis. The challenge of science as the here of technology. Amer. Psychol. 22: 118–130 (1967b).

HIRSCH, J.: Behavior-genetic analysis and its biosocial consequences. Seminars Psychiat. 2: 89–105 (1970).

HULL, C.: Principles of behavior (Appleton-Century, New York 1943).

HUNT, J. McV.: Has compensatory education failed? Has it been attempted? Harv. educ. Rev. 39: 278–299 (1969).

HUNT, J.: Intelligence and experience (Ronald, New York 1961).

JENSEN, A.: How much can we boost IQ and achievement? Harv. educ. Rev. 39: 1–123 (1969).

JENSEN, A.R.: Hebb's confusion about heritability. Amer. Psychol. 26: 394–395 (1971).

KAGAN, J.: The concept of intelligence. Humanist 32: 7–8 (1972).

KAMIN, L.J.: Heredity, intelligence; politics and psychology. Presentation delivered at Temple University, Philadelphia 1972.

KOHLBERG, L.: Early education. A cognitive-developmental view. Child Develop. 39: 1014–1062 (1968).

KUHN, T.S.: The structure of scientific revolutions; 2nd ed. (Univ. of Chicago Press, Chicago 1970).

LEHRMAN, D.S.: Semantic and conceptual issues in the nature-nurture problem; in ARONSON, TOBACH, LEHRMAN and ROSENBLATT Development and evolution of behavior, pp. 17–52 (Freeman, San Francisco 1970).

LIGHT, R.: Intelligence and genes. Humanist 32: 12–13 (1972).

LIGHT, R.J. and SMITH, P.V.: Social allocation models of intelligence. Harv. educ. Rev. 39: 484–510 (1969).

LIGHT, R.J. and SMITH, P.V.: Statistical issues in social allocation models of intelligence. A review and a response. Rev. educ. Res. *41:* 351–367 (1971).

LOEVINGER, J.: On the proportional contributions of differences in nature and in nurture to differences in intelligence. Psychol. Bull. *40:* 725–756 (1943).

LORENZ, K.: Evolution and the modification of behavior (Univ. of Chicago Press, Chicago 1965).

McCLELLAND, D.: IQ tests and assessing competence. Humanist *32:* 9–12 (1973).

NICHOLS, R.C.: The national merit twin study; in VANDENBERG Methods and goals in human behavior genetics, pp. 231–242 (Academic Press, New York 1965).

OVERTON, W.F. and REESE, H.W.: Models of development. Methodological implications; in NESSELROADE and REESE Life-span developmental psychology. Methodological issues, pp. 65–86 (Academic Press, New York 1972).

PEPPER, S.C.: World hypotheses (Univ. of California Press, Berkeley 1942).

PIAGET, J.: Biology and knowledge (Univ. of Chicago Press, New York 1971).

PIAGET, J. and INHELDER, B.: The psychology of the child (Basic Books, New York 1969).

PROSCH, H.: The genesis of twentieth century philosophy (Doubleday, New York 1964).

RATNER, C.: Principles of dialectical psychology. Telos *9:* 83–109 (1971).

REESE, H.W. and OVERTON, W.F.: Models of development and theories of development; in GOULET and BALTES Life-span developmental psychology. Research and theory, pp. 116–150 (Academic Press, New York 1970).

SCARR-SALAPATEK, S.: Race, social class and IQ. Science *174:* 1285–1295 (1971).

SHOCKLEY, W.: Negro IQ deficit. Failure of a 'malicious allocation' model warrants new research proposals. Rev. educ. Res. *41:* 227–248 (1971a).

SHOCKLEY, W.: Models, mathematics, and the moral obligation to diagnose the origin of negro IQ deficits. Rev. educ. Res. *41:* 369–377 (1971b).

SKEELS, H.M.: Adult status of children with contrasting early life experiences. Monogr. Soc. Res. Child Develop. *31:* (3): 1–66 (1966).

SKEELS, H.M. and DYE, H.B.: A study of the effects of differential stimulation of mentally retarded children. Proc. amer. Ass. ment. Deficiency *44:* 114–136 (1939).

SKINNER, B.F.: Beyond freedom and dignity (Knopf, New York 1971).

SPIKER, C.C.: The concept of development. Relevant and irrelevant issues; in STEVENSON Concept of development. Monogr. Soc. Res. Child Develop. *31:* (5): 40–54 (1966).

TANNER, J.M.: Physical growth; in MUSSEN Carmichael's manual of child psychology, vol. 1, pp. 77–156 (Wiley, New York 1970).

VANDENBERG, S.G.: The hereditary abilities study. Hereditary components in a psychological test battery. Amer. J. hum. Genet. *14:* 220–237 (1962).

WADDINGTON, C.H.: The theory of evolution today; in KOESTLER and SMYTHIES Beyond reductionism, pp. 357–374 (Beacon Press, Boston 1971).

WEISS, P.: The living system: determinism stratified; in KOESTLER and SMYTHIES Beyond reductionism, pp. 3–42 (Beacon Press, Boston 1971).

WHITE, S.H.: The learning-maturation controversy: Hall to Hull. Merrill-Palmer Quart. *14:* 187–196 (1968).

WOHLWILL, J.: The age variable in psychological research. Psychol. Rev. *77:* 49–65 (1970).

Request reprints from: Dr. WILLIS F. OVERTON, Department of Psychology, Temple University, *Philadelphia, PA 19122* (USA)

Human Develop. *16:* 90–107 (1973)

The Concept of Experience: S or R?

J. F. WOHLWILL

Pennsylvania State University, University Park, Pa.

Abstract. The term 'experience' has been used by developmental psychologists to refer both to effects of environmental stimulation and to opportunity for the acquisition of a particular behavior. This paper contrasts these differing conceptions of the role of experience and their consequences for various issues in this field. The two types of experiental effects are further expanded by considering the role of control, through selection and exploratory behavior, over environmental stimulation, and of feedback from the environment to the child's response. The relevance of the resulting fourfold scheme for a conceptualization of environmental effects in development is discussed and suggestions made for a functional ecology of development.

Key Words
Environment
Experience
Stimulation
Sensory experience
Feedback
Exploratory behavior
Ecology

One of the criticisms that environmentalists have been prone to level against those who would attribute a functional role to hereditary variables in human behavior is that they represent little more than a cloak for our ignorance, given the virtual impossibility, in the foreseeable future, of isolating the contribution of specific genes to behavior at the human level. Whether or not one accepts this argument on its merits – and it is a debatable one – it ignores the fact that the standard equation, $B = f(H, E)$ is in fact an equation in *two* unknowns. The fact is that environmentalists have, by and large, been woefully unspecific in their reference to the role of 'environment' as a determinant of behavior; particularly in the human differential psychology literature on the heredity-environment question, little consideration has typically been given to specifying the meaning of 'environmental' influences or of the variables presumed to be operating to mediate such influences. Environment has, in fact, represented a catchall for everything from mere opportunity for the exercise of a motor response to the broad complex of forces operating in the child's familial, social and cultural milieu. The term has been used interchangably to refer to ill-defined aspects of the physical, the interpersonal and the institutional environment, encompassing such diverse aspects as child-rearing practices, schooling and the trappings of our material civilization.

This diffuseness in our use of the term 'environment' and our thinking about its role in behavior is reflected in the basic ambiguity surrounding the closely related term 'experience', which has been at the core of the environmentalist's vocabulary. Upon even cursory examination, it appears that there is a remarkable lack of consistency in the use of this term, even with respect to as fundamental an issue as to whether it is intended to refer to a variable on the stimulus or the response side of the ledger.

This ambiguity is probably traceable to the similar looseness in the colloquial useage of this term. Thus, of the several definitions given in Webster (e.g., Webster's *New World Dictionary of the English Language,* College Edition), the first three or four, though couched in subjective and phenomenologically tainted language, clearly refer to forces, circumstances or events impinging on the individual from the outside, e.g., 'an actual living through an event or events ... anything observed or lived through ... all that had happened to one; everything that one has seen or done'. Yet subsequent definitions refer rather to overt behavior, i.e., 'activity that includes training, observation of practice and personal participation ... knowledge, skill, or practice resulting from this' – a use consonant with that commonly found in want-ads, or in the conversation in the bar or college dorm concerning sexual exploits.

What may be a forgivable lack of clarity or consistency in popular parlance becomes a potentially dangerous source of confusion when encountered in scientific use. To face the question squarely: when someone argues for the role of previous experience in the development of behavior, is he suggesting that certain antecedent *stimulus conditions* have been operative, which determined or affected the formation of that behavior, or is he referring to the influence of previous *responses,* elicited during the period in which the experience was in effect, on the individual's subsequent behavior?

There are undoubtedly those who would argue that this question is not a meaningful or reasonable one, for any of several reasons. A phenomenologist, for instance, would challenge the basic propriety of attempting a sharp differentiation between stimulus and response processes; to him 'experience' would consist of the individual's prior history of stimuli or events *as perceived and assimilated by him.* (As already noted, the nonbehaviorally oriented definitions in Webster are worded in similar phenomenological terms, as is that given in the *American College Dictionary* (6th ed.) for the philosoph-ical use of the term: 'the totality of the cognitions given by perception'.)

This particular objection, whatever its validity or force as a metatheoreti-cal issue, may be countered by noting that those who have most commonly addressed themselves to the role of experience in development have not done so from a phenomenological point of view, but have rather represented some variant of the empiricist position – whether strictly behavioristic [e.g., BIJOU and BAER, 1961; GEWIRTZ, 1969] or more friendly to cognitive analysis [e.g., HUNT, 1961]. These theorists might, however, raise a very different objection to the formulation of the S vs. R question as stated above, in either or terms. They might well argue that 'experience' represents a construct which en-compasses aspects of both S *and* R, in the sense that it refers to environ-mental conditions which provide an opportunity or context for certain responses, or conversely for a set of responses elicited within a given environmental context. Yet, as will be seen, such a tenuous fence-straddling position robs the concept of much of its usefulness; certainly it is of little value, either in planning research, whether in the laboratory or in the field, or in conceptualizing the manner in which known experiential effects on behavior actually operate.

For the fact is that as soon as one sets about to study the effects of some particular experience on development empirically, one is forced to choose sides; that is, the decision as to whether to treat the variables to be investi-gated in stimulus or response terms is thrust upon one. This point is brought out sharply by an examination of some of the prior research on this question, particularly as HUNT [1961] has reviewed it, in the context of the question to what extent intelligence is a fixed entity, or one modifiable by the indi-vidual's 'experience'.

Thus, if we look at HUNT's account of the literature on the maturation-learning question, predominantly dating back to the 30s, we find that this controversy deals for the most part with the role played by exercice of a given response on the later development of that or related responses. Here 'experience' refers quite explicitly to opportunity for practice, whether restricted or enhanced relative to the norm. It thus has an unambiguous status on the response side, i.e., the development of a particular behavior is made to appear (or not to appear, as the case may be) contingent on the occurrence of previous responses.

On the other hand, HUNT [1961] provides equally comprehensive coverage of research on the role of early *stimulus* experience, notably that inspired by HEBB's theory of early perceptual learning. Here 'experience' refers just as unmistakably to exposure to certain stimulus conditions, generally either 'enriching' or 'impoverishing' in relation to some assumed or established control level. In the theoretical accounts of this work no role is ascribed to any response which may have been elicited or inhibited during the stimulus-exposure period.

Lastly, a variety of studies cited by HUNT [1961], mostly of a non-experimental nature, treat experience in such global terms as to fail to differentiate between the two sides of the question, or to permit others to ascribe the observed effects to either stimulus or response factors. This is the case for such studies as the classical ones on the relationship between nursery-school experience and IQ, and those on the effects of institutionalization on intellectual development. It is true as well of some (although not all) of their contemporary equivalents – e.g., much of the research on the effects of compensatory education [HESS and BEAR, 1968]. Here no attempt is made to achieve control over the specific factors mediating the observed effects; thus either stimulus or response variables or, most typically, both of them in interaction, may have been operative.

This issue might be thought to be beside the point for work whose primary aim is to overcome the deleterious effects on development of early deprivation, or which has a similar practical goal. Yet we may refer to at least one instance of a social experiment for compensatory education on a massive scale that has, for purely practical reasons, restricted itself entirely to the stimulus side in devising the conditions of special experience on which it was to rely. This is the Television series, *Sesame Street,* which, along with its successor, *The Electric Company,* has earned the plaudits of psychologists, educators and parents alike. Inevitably, the approach of putting television to the service of compensatory education is predicated on a view of experience in which the primary emphasis is on exposure to stimuli, with little attention being given to the responses given to them.[1] It is possible to counteract this emphasis to an extent, as shown in the instructional use of the medium in developing particular skills, whether in the realm of physical exercice, self-defense, or cookery. In the case of *Sesame Street,* on the other hand, the

---

[1] As a participant in one of the seminars organized while *Sesame Street* was in the planning stage, this writer had occasion to discuss this aspect of the contemplated program with its staff, and suggested the possibility of distributing materials in kits to the prospective viewers, to which they might be induced to respond via the program. The notion was, however, dismissed as impractical to implement on the scale on which the program was intended.

thrust appears to be designed deliberately to minimize opportunity for overt responding by the child: not only is no attempt made to talk to the viewer, or to involve him in the action and stimulation in any role except that of a purely passive viewer, but the heavy reliance on a rapid-fire succession of discrete stimuli (as in the segments on particular letters of the alphabet) is likewise calculated to *prevent* differential responses by the viewer to the stimuli.

If the question as to the side of the stimulus-response ledger on which the concept of experience belongs is thus of direct consequence for the formulation of applied educational programs designed to provide special experience for children growing up under conditions of deprivation, it is obviously all the more critical at a theoretical level. Indeed, it sets apart HEBB and his followers, who have laid exclusive stress on sensory experience, from those, ranging from HELD and his associates to PIAGET, who in one way or another attribute a major role to the responses which the infant or young child makes to the world of stimuli around him. Unfortunately, while the argument between these opposing views can be readily enough joined, it is difficult to find conclusive evidence that would permit one to decide between them, for the simple reason that the requisite controls or ongoing monitoring of the individual's behavior during the course of the period of experimentally manipulated experience have rarely been included in the research plans. This limitation has been as characteristic of the experimental research in the animal laboratory, such as that inspired by HEBB, as it has at the human level in the work of such investigators as WHITE [1971], based on a combination of Heldian and Piagetian notions.

But it is not the intent of this paper to focus on these questions of methodology or design of research in this area called for to illuminate the question raised in the title, especially since the writer has dealt with these matters in a forthcoming publication [WOHLWILL, 1973b]. Rather, the balance of this paper will be devoted to sharpening the contrast between the two positions and to assess their respective places, along with certain variants of each, in the development of the child. Finally, the attempt will be made to apply this view of experience to a general ecological model for developmental psychology.

The Environment: Source of Stimulation Versus Context for Response

Undoubtedly, environments influence the development of a child in very diverse ways – a diversity which has generally been obscured by the polarity of the nativism vs. empiricism, heredity vs. environment and maturation vs. learning controversies. The preceding discussion suggests two alternative models of environmental effects, which, while by no means mutually exclusive, represent contrasting poles that are usefully differentiated, permitting us to consider particular situations as representing variants of each along specified dimensions. Let us examine them in greater detail.

Type I. The Environment as a Source of Stimulation

Here we are referring to the type of environmental effects emphasized by HEBB, i.e., those deriving directly from sheer exposure to stimuli. The accumulated evidence from the research inspired by HEBB's ideas has left no room for doubt as to the crucial importance of a context of patterned stimulation for normal perceptual, cognitive and even affective development, although, as already noted, the experimental conditions have by no means established unambiguously that it is stimulation *per se,* as opposed to the establishment of differential responses made possible by patterned stimulation, that is the primary factor implicated in these effects – leaving aside for the moment direct effect of sensory impoverishment on normal physiological functioning (e.g., the atrophy of retinal cells in blind-reared animals).

For the developmental psychologist, and the human developmental psychologist in particular, however, the central question raised by the Hebbian view is a very different one, namely: Can development be assumed to be a monotonic function of amount and diversity of environmental stimulation? Such a 'the more the merrier' view does indeed appear to be implied by HEBB's writing and the research it has inspired, notably in the bi-polar conception of the role of stimulation embodied in the 'enrichment' vs. 'impoverishment' distinction. Furthermore, most of the published enrichment literature has appeared to support this conception, in so far as the effects of enrichment have been found to yield positive enhancement of a variety of behavioral measures. But it must be remembered that the baseline for the 'enrichment' concept was that of the laboratory-raised rat; similarly, the baseline in WHITE's [1971, regimen of experience for the enhancement of infant development was represented by the environmental stimulation afforded by an institution.

The fact is that we know as yet very little concerning the effects of levels of stimulation at the pole opposite to that of the sensory deprivation experiment, whether studied in adults via short-term experience, or in the developing individual by manipulating conditions of early experience over an extended period of time [cf. WOHLWILL, 1973a]. It is important for us to know more, not only about the effects of increasing intensity and diversity of stimulation beyond the optimal level (assuming, as most theorists do, that an optimal-level hypothesis is tenable), but about the dimensions of the stimulus input that are of importance in this regard [cf. WOHLWILL, 1973a]. In particular we need to concern ourselves with the effect of stimulation to which the individual is unable to make differential responses, either because the input rate is beyond his capacity to process, or because it is devoid of meaning for him, i.e., he lacks the schemata to which he might relate the information. Note that this type of concern is quite foreign to a Hebbian view, which appears to take the information-processing aspect for granted. It may be suggested that it is of relatively less concern during HEBB's primary learning phase, in which the original perceptual schemata are being established, than in the secondary one, in which higher-order cognitive structures are built up.

One of the categories of stimulus input which surely deserves special attention is that which comes in the form of linguistic messages. Here again we have at least implicitly accepted a maximization principle, in emphasizing the stimulation of the child's verbal development through intensive verbal interaction with the mother, as well as the beneficial role of TV in this regard. But we need to know how much verbal stimulation the child can actually assimilate at a given age, and what the consequences are when that level is exceeded: is it possible that the child develops a tuning-out mechanism for dealing with the problem that may in fact interfere with optimal language development? Just such a mechanism has been proposed by MILGRAM [1970] as underlying adults' attempts to cope with the surfeit of social stimulation inherent in life in our large urban centers. The argument is admittedly a speculative one, but it does not seem implausible to invoke it as an element of the 'cultural deprivation' facing the slum child, living under crowded quarters highly permeable to the diffusion of auditory stimuli.

Type II. The Environment as a Context for Behavior

Much of the classical maturation-learning controversy dealt with environment essentially in this sense, i.e., as a setting that to varying degrees provided the opportunity for a child to engage in a particular response. Thus certain environments may promote the practice of certain motor skills, as in the well-known work of McGraw [1935] on Johnny and Jimmy; others may facilitate speech development (or hinder it), while still others may foster, or inhibit, social interaction. The determining environmental attributes in this regard may be aspects of the physical environment – e.g., a child growing up in a ranch house has comparatively little opportunity to learn to climb stairs; temperate climates, permitting outdoor activity the year around, favor the development of athletic talent, e.g., in such sports as swimming and tennis. Alternatively, they may refer to the interpersonal environment (e.g., the presence of a twin serves to inhibit the normal course of the child's acquisition of language through interaction with his mother and other significant adults and older sibs), or to the institutional environment: the existence and acceptance of preschool experience for the young child will affect his exposure to other children of his own age with whom he can interact. The essential common factor in all of these cases is the role of the particular environmental circumstances as modulators of the degree of opportunity afforded the child to engage in the response in question.

Types I and II Contrasted

The distinction between the two opposing conceptions of environmental effects just presented takes on a degree of face validity once we note some of the diverse respects in which the two types of effects appear to differ. Let us consider, in this regard, (a) the reversibility of the two effects; (b) the meaning of an 'optimal' environment with reference to each, and (c) the mode of interaction between heredity and environment in each case.

a) Reversibility. A case can be made for the proposition that the wonted 'primacy' of early experience applies mainly to experiential effects of type I. Compare, for instance, the well-known cases reported by SENDEN [1960] of patients born blind, who were given sight by a cataract operation some time during their later childhood or adolescence, with the effects of confinement and relative immobilization of children growing up in an orphanage [DENNIS, 1960]. While the latter did report marked motor retardation in the development of the children under these conditions of institutionalization, he likewise emphasizes that he did not find any older children who had not mastered the elementary skills of walking and the like. In contrast SENDEN's patients had great difficulty learning to see following their operations, and HEBB relied heavily on this evidence in formulating his theory of perceptual lerning.

The matter is not as clear-cut as one might wish, since the clinical evidence from SENDEN's cases is open to criticism on various grounds [e.g., WERTHEIMER, 1951], while the experimental literature at the animal level on the reversibility question is by no means wholly supportive [e.g., FULLER, 1967]. Furthermore, the work on the critical-period hypothesis dealing with the acquisition of specific behaviors in lower animals (i. e.,imprinting) has pointed to a degree of irreversibility of early experience in type II effects. Nevertheless, at the human level, and probably that of the higher mammals as well, the same factors that would, at least according to HEBB's view, enhance the potency of early stimulus experience (i.e., the A/S ratio of the brain) should be expected to reduce the importance of mechanisms of the imprinting type, and more generally the time- or maturation-dependent character for the acquisition of a particular behavior.

b) The 'optimal environment' concept. For environmental effects of type II, it would seem apparent that a maximization principle applies. If we wish to develop a particular skill in a child, be it to turn him into a skier or swimming champion, a prodigy on the violin, or a precocious reader, the development of that skill can be assumed to be a direct function of the extent of opportunity for the practice of that skill and positive encouragement of it that the environment provides the child. In contrast, as was already noted earlier, there is a strong presumption that an optimal-level notion applies in the realm of amount and intensity of stimulation provided in the child's early experience, and that an excess of stimulation may be as detrimental to optimal development as a deficiency of it. The question remains what the relevant dimensions of the stimulus input are along which deficiency and excess are to be considered. Surely intensity represents one such dimension; conceivably variety, particularly of overlapping sources of stimulation, does likewise.

Admittedly 'optimal development' means two rather different things in the case of environments I and II: in the first, the index would be some general measure of behavioral development, such as intelligence, developmental quotient, or the like, whereas in the second we are by definition dealing rather with a particular response. Indeed, it is conceivable that concentrated practice of a single motor or cognitive skill resulting in precocity of development in a narrow area may have unwonted side-effects in terms of the child's overall development, as suggested by the symptoms of emotional problems in FOWLER's daughter, following the intensive period of training in reading which she underwent at the age of two [FOWLER, 1962]. But here we are clearly dealing with *by-products* of the practice which the child's environment made possible, rather than with general effects of the experience *per se*.

A related difference with direct consequences for the very notion of the optimal environment concerns the different role played by adaptation processes in the two cases. As this writer has argued elsewhere [WOHLWILL, 1973a], there is a strong suggestion from the adult literature that the optimal-level of stimulation principle may in fact be the resultant of the operation of adaptation-level processes, which would typically ensure optimal performance (or maximal preference) corresponding to the intermediate levels of stimulation to which the average individual will generally have become become adapted. It is highly likely that a similar process applies to the effects of differential levels of stimulation in development, i.e., that the individual will tend to become adapted, within relatively wide limits, to whatever level characterized his own early environment, such that his later development may well be a function of the maintenance of that level, or conversely of the extent of discrepancy from it with which he is forced to cope. Note that such an interpretation is consonant with FULLER's [1967] emphasis on the stress to which an organism is exposed in emerging from an original isolation experience to a 'normal' environment, as the basis for observed behavioral deficits from such experience.

By contrast, on the response side adaptation processes of this sort do not seem to be demonstrable. To be sure, we do observe effects of habituation or desensitization with respect to the strength of a repeatedly elicited response, but here we are dealing with responses to specific eliciting stimuli. In the case of the acquisition of skills and similar responses such as considered under type II effects, on the other hand, the exercise of those skills appears rather to represent a self-generating process, i.e., the more often the response occurs, the greater the likelihood of its being repeated and further developed, owing presumably to the satisfaction and reinforcement which the child derives from its perfection and mastery.

c) The interaction between heredity and environment. As suggested at the outset of the paper, we are still some considerable distance from an effective mode of conceptualizing the role of hereditary factors in development, whether considered in themselves, or in interaction with environmental factors. One of the Hebbian studies [COOPER and ZUBEK, 1958] is, however, suggestive in this respect, since it appears to indicate that special environmental experience can in fact override genetic factors: A group of 'maze-bright' rats was equivalent in their maze performance to a group of 'maze-dull' rats, when both had been raised under either enrichment or restriction conditions; it was only for rats raised under normal-cage conditions that the difference due to heredity manifested itself. This study has generally been interpreted to point to the strong *interactive* nature of the operation of environmental and hereditary forces, i.e., that a depriving environment depressed the performance of the 'brights' to the level of the 'dulls', while an enriching environment enhanced the performance of the 'dulls' so as to bring it to the level of the 'brights'. But the salient fact from the data of COOPER and ZUBEK [1958] is simply that under either extreme environmental condition hereditary effects were obliterated.

We do not have similar data to report with respect to type II effects, and even with respect to those of type I, the COOPER and ZUBEK [1958] experiment provides admittedly a limited basis from which to draw any sweeping conclusions. Yet the possibility suggests itself that stimulus experience may have just such an overriding effect because of the non-specificity of its action, i.e., no particular response is implicated in its effects. On the other hand, in the case of type II effects one would expect a much more direct interactive effect between the operation of hereditary and environmental mechanisms, i.e., in the sense that the environmental context will determine to what extent the individual's genetic potential with respect to a particular response will in fact be manifested. The *interactive* pattern here applies due to the action of the environment in magnifying incipient hereditary differences with respect to a particular response: for instance, inherent differences in strength or musical talent between two children will tend to become reinforced as a result of the differential reinforcement of those skills by the environment, thereby providing differential encouragement for their further development.

Four Prototypes of Experiental Effects

It is to be anticipated that the foregoing distinction between environments of types I and II will be considered as a highly artificial one by many readers, useful at best for laboratory experimentation and for purely analytic purposes, but with little relationship to the 'real world'. Admittedly the notion of a child being 'bathed' in a world of stimulation in the sense of purely passive exposure, which appears to correspond to the Hebbian view, is both oversimplified and unwarranted, to the extent that it leaves out the behavioral response of the organism to this world of stimulation. As already noted earlier, most of the Hebbian research on the role of early experience has exerted little if any control on the overt behavior of the animal during the exposure period (except for certain studies in which motor restriction has been used as an experimental variable), and thus the possible contribution of motor activity to the effects of early-experience research (or its suppression under conditions of sensory restriction) remains unknown. By the same token, the role of environmental stimuli in providing support for or possibly inhibiting the acquisition of response skills as envisaged in type II effects can hardly be ignored: The learning of bicycling skills will be affected by an array of environmental factors ranging from the nature of the terrain, the availability of sidewalks and the conditions of traffic to the role of other cycling children to serve as models and possibly reinforcers of the behavior.

The distinction made may yet be a valuable one in defining what we may regard as opposite modes of conceiving the role of experience; by adding to them certain variants, we arrive at a more realistic scheme for categorizing environmental effects. Let us therefore expand our prior dichotomy of two environmental effects into a set of four prototypes, by introducing the concept of selective response to modify type I effects, and that of response-produced environmental change to modify type II effects. We will dub the resulting four prototypes as the model of the hospital bed, the model of the amusement park, the model of the tennis match and the model of the swim meet.

I. The 'hospital-bed' model of experience. This model is intended to refer to the relatively pure case of type I effects, where the individual is in effect the passive recipient of a complex and diversified regimen of stimulation over which he exerts only very limited control, and to which he makes few if any differential responses – as in the case of the patient confined to and immobilized in his bed, and at the extreme unable even through verbal means to control his environment, e.g., by asking to have the channel of his TV set changed. This model does seem to correspond to the world of the very young infant in his crib to a large degree, and it is probably this period during which most infants spend most of their time in the crib that HEBB appears to have in mind in his discussion of primary perceptual learning (though he has never been very explicit in his discussion of developmental periods, particularly as they would apply at the human level).

I'. The 'amusement-park' model of experience. Here the individual is surrounded by a world of stimulation characterized by variety and intensity, but he can, through his own behavior, direct his attention to one or another aspect or feature of this environment, while disregarding the rest. Note that to a large extent his control of the environment through his own behavior is limited to this selection effect: once he has decided to partake of the rollercoaster ride, there is little he can do to alter the experience he will derive from it. (Even in the case of the electric-car rides, the drivers have only minimal control over their environment; no matter how skillful or timorous, each is virtually assured his share of jarring collisions and jolts – which is of course precisely the basis for its attraction.)

II. The 'swim-meet' model of experience. Here we find the pure type II case, in which the environment serves merely as a constant context for the exercise of a response, or chain of responses. From the sound of the gun the individual's behavior takes its course in virtual independence from environmental stimuli (except for the constant constraints exerted by the temperature of the water, the length and shape of the pool, etc., as well as occasionally the position of other swimmers with which he is competing).

II'. The 'tennis-match' model of experience. The central feature of this model is the fact that the tennis player's behavior is locked into a tight feedback loop with his stimulus environment: not only are his responses directly determined by the state of that environment at any given moment (more specifically, by the movement of the ball, and the position of his adversary), but they create a change in that environment, and above all a response on the part of the environment to which he responds in turn. Much of children's play, e.g., in the nursery school, is of this sort, although the 'give and take' may not be as tightly determinate as a literal interpretation of this model would suggest.

The point of the foregoing presentation was to suggest how the two reference poles of purely passive exposure and purely autonomous behavior could be used as a framework for describing different kinds of experience in the developing child. Young infants do spend time in their cribs, engaged in essentially passive reception of their world of stimulation (and their slightly elder sibs similarly pass time 'glued' to the TV set, absorbing stimulation in a comparably passive fashion). Likewise, children do take part in swim-meets, and even younger children may engage in sustained behavior of a similarly autonomous sort, e.g., around a jungle gym. Yet most of the child's experience represents some degree of variation from these two extremes, involving elements of exploration and/or selection of stimuli, as in the amusement-park model, or of stimulus-behavior feedback, as in the tennis-match model, and quite possibly some combination of these.

Is it possible to order these four prototypes along a continuum? If so, we should be able to specify some type of environmental experience located in the middle, in the sense of involving approximately equal parts of stimulus exposure, selected though not directly controlled by or differentially responded to by the individual, and of semi-autonomous behavior to which the environment responds. The initial experience of the child upon entering nursery school might perhaps be looked at in this fashion, involving as it does exposure to a whole set of new stimuli over which the child can exert only a modicum of control, but along with an opportunity to engage in active behavior (e.g., 'free play') which may produce a response in his social environment, that is, on the part of other children, or adults. But are we dealing here with a mixture of two basically different types of experience, such as would warrant retaining the qualitative dichotomy between types I and II, or does this case constitute a true integration of the two types, thereby justifying the postulation of a dimension varying from one to the other? This question is difficult to answer categorically, but the preference of this writer is for the former view, stipulating exposure to stimulation and free response as qualitatively separate types of experience, the former modulated by selection and exploration, and the latter by stimulus-response feedback loops, but remaining withal two distinct modes of experience.

Towards a Functional Ecology of Behavioral Development

What role does each of the aforementioned models of environmental experience play in the child's development? Is this role itself subject to change during the course of development? Is there some kind of ideal composite mixture of them that could be considered to represent an optimal experience? Answers to these questions, apart from having obvious practical implications, would help contribute to a developmental theory formulated in terms of the changing mode of the child's interaction with his environment, and could thus pave the way towards a functional ecology of development, to complement the descriptive kind which BARKER, WRIGHT and their colleagues have provided for us [cf. WRIGHT, 1956].

To begin with, although it might be tempting to postulate a developmental shift from reliance on type I experience in infancy and early childhood to a primacy of type II in maturity (i.e., from passive exposure to environmentally autonomous behavior), this would surely be a vastly oversimplified view. To begin with, from the time that the infant acquires a repertoire of voluntary motor responses he becomes involved in type II experience; at the same time to some degree the individual continues to absorb stimulation in the passive sense of type I experience throughout his life, and for all we know not without some benefit to the development and maintenance of his behavior.

Rather than viewing development as a simple shift from type I to II, it appears more profitable to look at these as independent varieties of environmental effects, each subject to its own change. First, in the realm of type I effects, we may assume a progressive increase over the course of infancy and early childhood in the role of selection and environmental exploration – thus a move from model I to I'; second, in the realm of type II effects, we may postulate a decreasing dependence on environmental feedback at least in later childhood – thus a move from model II' to II.

The implication of this analysis is that the environment may be beneficial to the child to the extent that it provides (a) opportunity for voluntary selection and exploration of environmental stimuli for passive exposure, so as to allow the child a measure of control over the rate of incoming information to be processed at a given time, as well as over the intensity, diversity and novelty of stimulation to which he is exposed, and (b) feedback to the child's own behavior, to foster environmentally adaptive and responsive behavior, as a foundation on which eventual autonomous behavior can develop.

These thoughts are clearly speculative, and, some might object, gratuitous. Yet they are not without support from both empirical research and the views of others. Thus, as regards the emphasis on voluntary exploration, we find that, given the opportunity, the child from a very early age (i.e., 9 months) will actively locomote to keep a source of stimulation in view, and will do so differentially in response to particular characteristics of the stimuli [SMITH et al., 1963]. The work of RHEINGOLD and ECKERMAN [1969] has further demonstrated, not only the propensity for exploration of unfamiliar environments by infants, but the way in which the presence of the mother modulates the manifestation of this behavior. At the same the importance of letting the child himself modulate the level of stimulation in his environment is suggested by the mounting evidence pointing to an optimal-level-of-stimulation (at least in terms of *preferred* levels in voluntary choice situations). The developmental picture in this respect is admittedly inconclusive at this moment (cf. THOMAS, 1966; MUNSINGER and KESSEN, 1966; WOHLWILL, 1971]; yet the optimal level concept appears on the face of it particularly appropriate to the child's early years, though it is unfortunately the very period (e.g., from later infancy through the preschool years) for which least hard evidence is available. [2]

From a different vantage point, and without benefit of direct empirical evidence, various writers concerned with the role of our urban environment in the development and maintenance of behavior have stressed the opportunity for exploration, and the presence of diversity and complexity in the environment as conducive to effective learning on the part of the child [PARR, 1966], as well as to environmental satisfaction on the part of the adult [RAPOPORT and KANTOR, 1967; PARR, 1966]. The question that arises here is whether our contemporary urban environment represents a positive or a negative force in this respect. Some [e.g., PARR, 1966] have stressed the lack of diversity of our urban environments, as well as the obstacles in the way of independent exploration of his environment by a young child growing up, for instance, in a large apartment house in Manhattan. Others [e.g., RAPOPORT and KANTOR, 1967] have emphasized instead the positive value of diversity and complexity characterizing our cities. The answer is clearly not a simple one, but one might suggest that some kind of happy medium might apply here, so that an optimal environment might be that of an intermediate-sized urban area, large enough to contain an effective amount of diversity, yet small enough to permit and encourage independent exploration from a fairly early age.

Turning to the other side of the picture, the beneficial role of environmental feedback has been recognized in most realms of the child's experience. It is embodied in the concept of the 'responsive environment', basic to the approach of MOORE and ANDERSON [1968] to early education; we find it in the realm of language learning in the role that recent developmental psycholinguistics has ascribed to various forms of adults' response to children's

---

[2] A most recent dissertation by MILBRATH [1972] provides some suggestive data on the role of self-pacing of the stimulus input in early experience at the animal level, although only in terms of measures of perceptual development. MILBRATH [1972] found that animals raised in a self-paced environment developed greater sensitivity to variations in light and tilt than animals receiving an equivalent amount of stimulation but without control over its onset and termination.

speech, such as 'expansion', 'prompting', 'modeling', and 'echoing' [BROWN *et al.,* 1968], and most obviously in the world of play, both individual and social. Little direct evidence exists to indicate the differential effects of different amounts of such feedback for the development of the child, but analyses of the ghetto experience in terms of a predominantly unidirectional mode of verbal interaction between parent and child, i.e., dominated by commands and closed-ended sentences [e.g., MILNER, 1951; JOHN and GOLDSTEIN, 1964; BERNSTEIN, 1961], are clearly consonant with the present view.

At the same time the suggestion that direct, sustained and immediate feedback to the individual for each response made by him becomes less essential over the course of development has at least surface plausibility. It appears to correspond to the course of developmental change in perceptual learning [WOHLWILL, 1966], and may well be applicable to such aspects of behavior as social learning and personality development (e.g., the progress from imitation to internalization in the identification process, and the movement from dependence to autonomy).

If we apply this analysis to the environmental settings in which development actually takes place, it is apparent that we are dealing here less with physical variables and more with interpersonal and institutional ones. By and large, our physical environment necessarily confronts the child with an essentially rigid, unresponsive context for behavior. The case of vehicular traffic represents a good illustration of this point: the child has to learn, for his own safety, to treat traffic as an environmental element virtually unresponsive to his own movements – though it would seem that California residents constitute a privileged class in this respect. Although in certain limited areas, and in special environments considered on a smaller scale, such as the classroom, this situation can be altered through appropriate technological means (e.g., computer-based auto-instructional devices), for the most part feedback from the environment emanates from other individuals, whether they be the child's peers or his elders.

Conclusion

The preceding discussion of optimal environments, and the attempt to formulate a functional developmental ecology of behavior may have the effect of detracting from what was intended as the main point of this paper. It is worth reiterating it, therefore, in closing. The concepts of 'environment' and 'experience' have generally been used all too loosely by psychologists, subsuming under them what are in fact very disparate kinds of effects. In particular, experience in the stimulation sense should be differentiated from experience in the behavioral sense; both of these undoubtedly play a major role in the development of the individual, but they operate in different ways, and are subject to different laws. This is not to say that any particular case of an experiential effect can be neatly classified into one or the other of these two categories – for instance, it is apparent that an experience such as 'nursery-school attendance' represents a mixture of both, as do other similarly complex (or perhaps simply ill-defined) kinds of experiences, such as 'institutional upbringing', 'cultural deprivation', etc. But little progress will be made in understanding such effects of experience until a more analytic approach is taken to defining their essential character. The typology suggested in this paper is intended with this purpose in mind.

References

BERNSTEIN, B.: Social class and linguistic development. A theory of social learning; in A.H. HALSEY, J. FLOUD and C.A. ANDERSON. Education, economy and society (Free Press, Glencoe 1961).

BIJOU, S.W. and BAER, D.M.: Child development. A systematic and empirical theory, vol. 1 (Appleton Century Crofts, New York 1961).

BROWN, R.; CAZDEN, C., and BELLUGI, U.: The child's grammar from I to III; in J.P. HILL. Minnesota symposium on child psychology, vol. 2 (Univ. of Minnesota Press, Minneapolis 1968).

CARR, S. and LYNCH, K.: Where learning happens. Daedalus 97: 1277–1291 (1968).

COOPER, R.M. and ZUBEK, J.P.: Effects of enriched and restricted environments on the learning ability of bright and dull rats. Canad. J. Psychol. 12: 159–164 (1958).

DENNIS, W.: Causes of retardation among institutional children. Iran. J. genet. Psychol. 96: 47–59 (1960).

FOWLER, W.: Teaching a two-year old to read. An experiment in early childhood learning. Genet. Psychol. Monogr. 66: 181–283 (1962).

FULLER, J.L.: Experiential deprivation and later behavior. Science 158: 1645–1652 (1967).

GEWIRTZ, J.L.: Mechanisms of social learning. Some roles of stimulation and behavior in early human development; in D.A. GOSLIN Handbook of socialization theory and research, pp. 57–212 (Rand McNally, Chicago 1969).

HESS, R.D. and BEAR, R.M.: Early education. Current theory, research and action (Aldine, Chicago 1968).

HUNT, J. McV.: Intelligence and experience (Ronald, New York 1961).

JOHN, V.P. and GOLDSTEIN, L.S.: The social context of language acquisition. Merrill-Palmer Quart. 10: 265–276 (1964).

McGRAW, M.B.: Growth. A study of Johnny and Jimmy (Appleton Century Crofts, New York 1935).

MILBRATH, C.: The consequences of a self-paced environment on perceptual development (Abstract). Diss. Abstr. Internat. *32 (B):* 4900 (1972).

MILGRAM, S.: The experience of living in cities. Science *167:* 1461–1468 (1970).

MILNER, E.: A study of the relationship between reading readiness in grade one school children and patterns of parent-child interaction. Child Develop. *22:* 95–112 (1951).

MOORE, O.K. and ANDERSON, A.R.: The responsive environments project; in R.D. HESS and R.M. BEAR Early education. Current theory, research and action (Aldine, Chicago 1968).

MUNSINGER, H. and KESSEN, W.: Stimulus variability and cognitive change. Psychol. Rev. *73:* 164–178 (1966).

PARR, A.A.: Psychological aspects of urbanology. J. soc. Issues *22 (4):* 39–45 (1966).

RAPOPORT, A. and KANTOR, R.E.: Complexity and ambiguity in environmental design. J. Amer. Inst. Planners *33:* 210–222 (1967).

RHEINGOLD, H.L. and ECKERMAN, C.O.: The infant's free entry into a new environment. J. exp. Child Psychol. *8:* 271–283 (1969).

SENDEN, M. VON: Space and sight. The perception of space and shape in the congenitally blind before and after operation (Tr. by P. HEATH) (Free Press, Glencoe 1960).

SMITH, K.U.; ZWERG, C., and SMITH, N.J.: Sensory-feedback analysis of infant control of the behavioral environment. Percept. mot. Skills *16:* 725–732 (1963).

THOMAS, H.: Preferences for random shapes. Ages six through nineteen years. Child Develop. *37:* 843–859 (1966).

WERTHEIMER, M.: HEBB and SENDEN on the role of learning in perception. Amer. J. Psychol. *64:* 133–137 (1951).

WHITE, B.L.: Human infants. Experience and psychological development (Prentice Hall, Englewood Cliffs 1971).

WOHLWILL, J.F.: Perceptual learning. Annu. Rev. Psychol. *17:* 201–232 (1966).

WOHLWILL, J.F.: Developmental evidence on the difference between specific and diversive exploration. Proc. Meet. Soc. Res. in Child Development. Minneapolis 1971.

WOHLWILL, J.F.: Behavioral response and adaptation to environmental stimulation (unpublished ms.)

WOHLWILL, J.F.: The study of behavioral development (in press, Academic Press, New York 1973b).

WRIGHT, H.F.: Psychological development in Midwest. Child Develop. *27:* 265–286 (1956).

Request reprints from: Dr. JOACHIM F. WOHLWILL, Division of Man-Environment Relations, Pennsylvania State University, *University Park, PA. 16802* (USA)

Human Develop. *16:* 108–118 (1973)

Infant Intelligence Tests: Their Use and Misuse[1]

M. Lewis

Educational Testing Service, Princeton, N.J.

Abstract. Data from a variety of infant intelligence test scores make clear that it is not possible to consider (1) that infant intelligence is a measurable, stable and unitary construct, (2) that there is a general g factor easily discernible in infancy, (3) that there is stability of scores both within and across scales, or (4) that there is predictability across age. These facts are discussed for their implications for models of intelligence, the use of intelligence tests in infancy, and finally intervention programs. It is concluded that the implicit model of general intelligence rests upon its function for society rather than its scientific merit. An alternative model of infant development is offered which is related to the acquisition of specific skills, the learning of which is dependent upon the match between the subject and the nature of the learning experience.

Key Words
Infancy
Intelligence
Subject-treatment interaction
Intervention

The concept of intelligence, the belief that it is relatively easily measurable, and that, as a monolithic construct, it is a useful predictor of subsequent human behavior, is firmly engrained in the mind of Western man. The consequence of this is to render a discussion of this construct difficult.

Using the data from a wide variety of infant and young children's tests of intelligence, we shall attempt to review the support for this construct. We will first demonstrate that infant intelligence as a measurable, stable and unitary construct is without foundation in fact. There is no general g factor easily discernible in infancy, no stability of scores both within and across scales, and no predictability. The only way to understand why this information, which has been known in part before, has gone unheeded is to observe both the uses and function of IQ scores in a technological society.

[1] This research was supported by a grant from the National Science Foundation, GB 8590.

The overall theme of this discussion rests upon two points: there is no demonstrable construct as infant intelligence, and early intervention procedures have failed to adequately test their effectiveness because they have neither taken the measurement issues into consideration nor the subject-treatment interaction. From these points of view the implicit model of general intelligence rests upon its function for society rather than its scientific merit. An alternative model of infant development is offered which is related to the acquisition of specific skills, the learning of which is dependent upon the match between the subject and the nature of the learning experience.

Is Infant Intelligence a Measurable, Stable and Unitary Construct?

In common with many others, BURT *et al.* [1934] expressed a view of intelligence as a finite potential with which the individual was endowed at conception, the manifestations of which increased at a stable rate during the growth process but which was subject neither to qualitative change nor to environmental influence. '...it is inherited or at least innate, not due to teaching or training. It is intellectual, not emotional or moral and remains uninfluenced by industry or zeal.' Moreover, BURT *et al.* [1934] held that intelligence could be measured with accuracy and ease. It is a *sine qua non* of such a view that measures of intelligence have high predictive validity from one age to another. Such validity is singularly lacking from every instrument used to assess intelligence during infancy. BAYLEY [1933] employing the first version of her infant developmental scales reports very little correlation between scores at 1, 2 and 3 months and scores at 18–36 months. These correlations range between 0.04 and 0.09.

McCALL *et al.* [1972] observed the stability and growth of intelligence in a sample of infants seen in the Fels Longitudinal Sample. Correlations of the Gesell scores in infancy were compared with childhood Stanford-Binet full-scale scores. The results, both for boys and girls, demonstrated that there was relatively little correlational relationship between the Gesell tests and the Stanford-Binet scores. McCALL *et al.* [1972] went on to construct a correlational matrix using data from a variety of different investigations. The results compare the relationship of IQ on a variety of infant tests with a variety of childhood tests. The data for over eight different reported studies reveal that there is almost no relationship between the first 12 months of life and subsequent test performance (the highest correlation accounts for just about 10% of the variance). The highest correlation, 0.54, accounts for less than 30% of the variance between any two ages. The authors conclude that in the first 3 years of life there is relatively poor prediction in infant tests of intelligence to IQ scores assessed in middle or late childhood. McCALL *et al.* [1972] went to great pain to find individual or factor item stability across tests and age; nevertheless, they were forced to conclude that even with this type of analysis and the use of a variety of other multivariate techniques, the correlational relationship between different ages 'remains modest and of minimum practical utility.' In conclusion, they reject the simple conceptualization of a g factor in infancy. 'The search for correlational stability across vastly different ages implies a faith in a developmentally constant, general conception of intelligence that presumably governs an enormous variety of mental activities. Under that assumption, the nature of the behavioral manifestations of g would change from age to age, but g itself is presumed constant, and this mental precocity at one age should predict mental precocity at another. Confronted with the evidence reviewed above, this g model of mental development must be questioned [McCALL *et al.,* 1972, p. 736].'

Perhaps if we turn from standardized kinds of tests, such as the Bayley or Gesell, to more recent approaches suggested by the Geneva school, we could find stability of infant mental ability. It may be necessary to utilize Piagetian theory and explore tasks more closely related to sensorimotor development to find stability and consistency. KING and SEEGMILLER [1971] applied the HUNT and UZGIRIS scales of perceptual cognitive development [1966] to 14-, 18- and 24-month-old infants. This test for the measurement of sensorimotor development consists of seven scales. The consistency of scores on these seven scales was compared across three ages as was the relationship at 14 months across the different scales. Not only did the authors find relatively little consistency in terms of the correlational scores (only 4 out of 24 possible correlations were significant) but also relatively little consistency across the various scales. Thus, even when we consider the non-standard intelligence tests and look at sensorimotor development, at least as measured by the HUNT and UZGIRIS scales [1966], we find no evidence for a consistency across age nor a g factor.

LEWIS and McGURK [1972] obtained and related three different types of infant intelligence tests. Infants were seen longitudinally from 3- to 24-months at which time they received the BAYLEY scales of infant development [1969] and the object permanence scale from the ESCALONA and CORMAN sensorimotor scales [1967]. In addition, at 24 months the children received the modified Peabody picture vocabulary test in which both a comprehension and production language score were obtained. For the Bayley scales the inter-age correlations proved to be relatively weak. Only two were significant and both of them accounted for less than 30% of the variance. The same was true for the object permanence scales of sensorimotor development. Out of a possible 15 correlations across the 3–24 months only two were significant and they accounted for less than 25% of the variance. Like the Bayley scores there was no clear across age pattern in the infant's performance on a sensorimotor function. LEWIS and McGURK [1972] then observed the correlations between the Bayley and object permanence scales at each age and between language development at 24 months and the Bayley and object permanence scores at each age. The results indicated an interesting developmental pattern. First, the Bayley scales were most closely related to the object permanence scales of the sensorimotor task in the first 6 months of life, while the Bayley scales were most closely related to language at 18 and 24 months. This result makes good sense. The early items from the Bayley scales are closely related to sensorimotor function, while the later Bayley items are related to language. And finally, and most important for our discussion, there was no significant relationship between the object permanence scales of sensorimotor functioning at any age and language ability at 24 months.

These three recent papers [McCALL *et al.,* 1972; KING and SEEGMILLER, 1971; LEWIS and McGURK, 1972] seem both to extend and reinforce earlier findings and support several broad conclusions concerning intellectual function during infancy. (1) Within a wide variety of standardized tests such as the Bayley and Gesell there is relatively little inter-age consistency in test performance during the first 2 years of life. Thus, children who are precocious at one age are not necessarily precocious at another. Moreover, early precociousness in the first 2 years seems to be unrelated to childhood performance on standard IQ tasks. (2) Non-standardized tests, constructed out of a Piagetian framework of sensorimotor development, also fail to show any consistency within the first 2 years of life. Thus, high scores on object permanence at one age do not necessarily mean that the child will have high scores on the object permanence at other ages. (3) Even within a particular age the results of both KING and SEEGMILLER [1971] and LEWIS and McGURK [1972] fail to indicate consistency across different measures of intellectual functioning; for example, there is little relationship between the Bayley scales and object permanence scales. Moreover, within age there is no consistency for tests such as the various sensorimotor scales of HUNT and UZGIRIS [KING and SEEGMILLER, 1971] or across different factors such as those found by McCALL *et al.* [1972] for the Gesell scales.

These results, as well as those reviewed by THOMAS [1970], STOTT and BALL [1965], and BAYLEY [1970], support the position that there is no consistency across or within age in a wide variety of tests purported to measure infant mental functioning. Therefore, the conception of a developmentally constant general intelligence is not a very tenable hypothesis.

Uses of Infant IQ Scores

What do these conclusions imply for the notion of intelligence which has been argued to be 'inherited or at least innate, not due to teaching or training and remains uninfluenced by industry or zeal [BURT *et al.,* 1934].' Such a model of human capacity must clearly be dealt a severe blow from a review of the infancy literature. And yet, such a conception of man remains. While these intelligence scales have thus been acknowledged to have limited functions, they are still widely used in clinical settings in the belief that, although lacking in predictive validity, they provide a valuable aid in assessing the overall health and developmental status of babies at the particular time of testing. This procedure is justified only if in the interpretation of such scores they are regarded solely as measures of present performance and not as indices of future potential. What this performance may mean is questionable since it is possible that superior performance may be indicative of subsequent poor performance. For example, BAYLEY [1955] shows a negative correlation of 0.30 between males early in test behavior and IQ at 16–18 years. Thus, infant scales are quite invalid as measures of future potential and it is also unlikely that they properly assess a child's current performance vis-à-vis the other children.

Currently, intelligence test scores are widely used as the criterion measure in the evaluation of infant intervention or enrichment programs. The experimental subjects are compared to the control subjects in terms of their performance on intelligence tests. If the scores of the experimental group are higher than those of the control, the program is evaluated positively; if not it is evaluated negatively. Implicitly assumed is that infant intelligence is a general unitary capacity and that mental development can be enhanced as a result of the enrichment experience in a few specific areas. Similarly, it is assumed that infant scales are adequate to reflect any improvement that occurs in competence as a consequence of a specific enrichment experience. However, infant intelligence as a general unitary capacity is highly questionable. Moreover, that infant scales are adequate to reflect improvement in specific enrichment experiences must also be highly questioned since both across and within consistency of a variety of infant skills tested show relatively little intra-scale consistency.

Thus, the data on infant intelligence tests also cast doubt on whether the scores have any generalizability beyond the particular set of abilities or factors sampled at the time of testing. An infant who showed dramatic gains in tasks involving sensorimotor functions would not necessarily manifest such gains in tests involving verbal skills. The implications of these conclusions for a wide variety of evaluative policies concerning infant intervention must be considered. For example, infant intelligence scales, no matter how measured, are quite unsuitable instruments for assessing the effects of specific intervention procedures, primarily, because infant intelligence cannot be considered a general unitary trait but is rather a composite of skills and abilities which do not necessarily covary. Such a view of intelligence is by no means new [see, for example, GUILFORD, 1959], but it is one which must be repeatedly stated in order to counteract the tendency to utilize simple and single measures of infant intelligence. An example will clarify this issue.

Consider an intervention procedure primarily intended to influence sensorimotor intelligence, for example, the development of object permanence.

An appropriate curriculum might involve training infants in a variety of peek-a-boo and hide-and-seek tasks. According to the data presented, a standard infant intelligence scale would be the wrong instrument to use in assessing the efficiency of such a program and is likely to lead to erroneous conclusions concerning the program's efficiency. Even more serious is the possibility that by using the wrong instrument of evaluation over a large number of programs one would erroneously conclude that intervention in general is ineffective in improving intellectual ability, thus supporting the genetic bias that environment is ineffective in modifying intelligence. There are few who would suggest that school children should be administered a standard intelligence test after a course in geography, yet such a procedure would be exactly analogous to using an intelligence test to measure the success of teaching the object concept to the young infant. The success of a geography course is best assessed by testing geographical knowledge and understanding and by the same token the success of a program stressing sensorimotor skills is best assessed by specific tests of sensorimotor ability. In both cases there may in some instances be improvement in intelligence test scores but such improvement has to be regarded as fortuitous.

The Function of IQ Scores

BURT'S [1934] view cannot be supported by the data. Why then should this view of intelligence hold such a dominant position in the thinking of contemporary scientists and public alike? The answer to such a question may be found by considering the function or use of the IQ score in a technological society. The function of the IQ score is and has always been to help stratify society into a hierarchy. The purpose of this hierarchy is to create a division of labor within the culture. That is, to determine who will go to school in the first place, who will get into academic programs that lead to college, etc. These divisions in turn determine the nature of labor the child will perform as an adult. This division of labor, a necessity in a complex society, is then justified by scores on a test designed to produce just such a division. If we cannot make the claim that IQ differences at least in infancy are genetically determined, then we must base them on differences in cultural-learning. But these differences, for the sake of the division of labor, are exactly what the IQ tests are intended to produce. The hierarchy of labor is maintained by the genetic myth. The hierarchy produces the test differences and the test differences are used to maintain the hierarchy. Thus,

IQ scores have come to replace the caste systems or feudal systems which previously had the function of stratifying society. Wherein these latter systems were supported by evoking the Almighty, the present system evokes Mother Nature. Undoubtedly, some sort of social stratification is necessary. We must find alternative means of achieving it.

An Interactionalist Approach

There are, of course, alternative views to BURT'S [1934] genetic position. In the present discussion and for the sake of increasing the range of considerations we shall take a totally interactionalist view – namely, that experience is both necessary for and the material of knowledge [LEWIS and LEE-PAINTER, 1972]. Like most interactionalists, we hold that intelligence (cognitive structures) is the consequence of action in the world and it is influenced by experience.

Cognitive structures are a consequence of interaction for adaptation and it is reasonable to suggest that they are influenced by the nature of the interaction itself. This kind of theorizing suggests an explanation for several different and divergent phenomena. First, it may help to explain individual and cultural differences in thought processes [COLE et al., 1971]. Second, it may explain why certain kinds of structures or groupings of structures are no longer capable of maintaining equilibrium. That is, if the world in which assimilation and accommodation take place changes, then the old structures or groupings are no longer adaptive in dealing with what is presently occurring. Thus, rather than emphasizing the genetic underpinning as the pressure for consistent change, we evoke the consistent pressures of the world. Although these are not specifiable at the moment neither are the genetic substrates which evoke the consistency both across the developmental sequence and people. We chose then to avoid relying on a nativist approach (some type of prewiring of sequence) and instead argue for an environmental organismic interaction in the process of development.

The effect of the infant's environment may make even more of a difference when we consider other cognitive structures, those which do not fit under a logical-mathematical framework, that is, space, volume, time, etc., as well as noncognitive structures. The infant and young child certainly develop structures about their social world through assimilation and accommodation. Unlike the logical-mathematical dimensions the specific attributes of the social world are as yet undefined, but there is reason to believe that these structures are affected by what the infant assimilates and accommodates to. For example, each time one infant vocalizes its mother vocalizes back, while for another infant vocalization produces a smile or look. For these two infants their vocalizations produce two worlds – one of vocalization, one of smiling. What is the effect, if any, on the child's resulting cognitive and noncognitive structures? Can we maintain that the resulting structure, infant action-outcome, will be invariant to either condition? Is it possible that in both examples the infant develops the knowledge of its mother (through responsivity toward him), but the nature of that knowledge is related to the specific behaviors directed toward it? We believe that the structures (intelligence), both in the cognitive and in the socioemotional realms of knowing must be affected by the environment in which the structures are formed.

The implications of such an interactionalist position can be seen most clearly in how we might organize our intervention programs – that is, change the environment to effect intellectual changes in the infant, and how to measure these changes [LEWIS, 1972].

Implications for Intervention Programs

It has been argued that the success or failure of intervention programs in early childhood and infancy is an indicator of the effect of environment on the intellectual growth and capacity of the child. If a variety of intervention programs are shown to be ineffective, then intervention or environment *per se* are ineffective in altering the intellectual performance capability of the infant or young child. If on the other hand, the intervention procedures are effective, then environment and changes in environment are a useful tool for altering intellectual performance capabilities. This would support a learning position in terms of the development of intelligence. The use of intervention then becomes highly relevant in discussing the issue of infant intelligence. Indeed, one might argue that this is one important method for getting at the effectiveness of environment on the infant's intellectual capacity. From an extreme interactionalist point of view the infant's intellectual capability is determined by the environment in which he exists. Thus, intervention programs should be crucial in determining whether or not this is the case.

We have already discussed the problems of measuring the effects of intervention by pointing out that infant intelligence cannot be considered some

unitary construct measured by a single instrument. Moreover, it is necessary
to match the evaluation of the intervention with the appropriate instrument.
Thus, if one were affecting object permanence capacity in the young infant
by such interventions as peek-a-boo games and showing the children how
to find hidden objects, then the type of measurement should *not* be the
Peabody picture vocabulary test or some other verbal task, but rather a
specific measure of sensorimotor capacity such as the object permanence
scales developed by HUNT and UZGIRIS [1966] or ESCALONA and CORMAN
[1967]. Note that KING and SEEGMILLER'S [1971] results would argue against
using the entire sensorimotor scales since they are not all necessarily related
to object permanence. Thus, if we are to use intervention programs as a
means of assessing whether infant's intellectual ability is fixed and unalter-
able by environment that we match the nature of the intervention procedure
to the criterion of effectiveness. This unfortunately is rarely done.

Of even more importance is the notion that all children can benefit from
the same kind of intervention procedure. This is a naive view, yet unfortunately it is widely held. Under this model every child in an intervention
procedure must receive the same treatment, either for the sake of 'scientific
objectivity' or technical simplicity. Thus, every child is to watch a particular
TV program or be instructed about a particular concept using a particular
set of instructional material. The popularity of this model is surprising since
both the educational experience in the classroom and more recently the
educational psychology literature have increasingly realized that children
need *different* types of intervention programs to arrive at the *same* goal,
because children come into the intervention procedure with different kinds
of experience. In the educational literature this issue refers to the aptitude-
treatment interaction or subject-treatment interaction. In order to reach the
same goal it is often necessary to apply different kinds of interventions (have
various curricula), dependent upon the characteristics of the child. In a
recent review, BERLINER and CAHEN [1973] make a strong argument for this
position in educational programs and, more importantly, in the evaluation
of their effectiveness. It is important to remember that it is the evaluation
of environment effectiveness which is one way to consider the effectiveness
of learning on the child's intellectual capacity.

An example of how we create difficulties by not considering the subject-
treatment interaction in evaluating the effectiveness of the child's experience
in the intervention program is necessary. Assume that we have 100 children
in intervention program A and that 10% of these children show increases
in some measurement of the effectiveness of the intervention A. 90% show

no effect or even show some negative effect of intervention A. When we look at the data of the experimental group, averaged over all 100 children, we must conclude that intervention A was not a success. If we have ten different intervention programs, each of them helping a different 10% of the experimental group, we would conclude that each of these programs failed to affect the measured capacity of these 100 children. Thus, intervention *per se* seems ineffective in influencing the child's intellectual capacities. In fact, this was not the case. All ten intervention programs succeeded in affecting the child's intellectual capacity but did not do so for the group as a whole. Thus, across all ten programs all 100 children's intellectual capacities, at least those that were designed to be affected by the intervention procedures, did show improvement. However, when we look at mean data we cannot locate any significant positive effect.

This example argues most powerfully for a subject-treatment interaction design both in terms of the nature of the program to be used and in terms of the evaluation of the effectiveness of that program.

It becomes then the function of the experimenter, curriculum developer, evaluator and finally theoretician to find what conditions each individual child needs to optimize his intellectual capacity. It is implicit in this assumption that (1) it is possible to find such conditions and that (2) having found such conditions we can come close to minimizing differences in intellectual capacity. Until such a program is initiated and until such a philosophy is undertaken, it is not fair to conclude that the intervention *per se* is ineffective or further that intellectual capacities cannot be affected by environmental change.

References

BAYLEY, N.: Mental growth during the first three years. A developmental study of sixty-one children by repeated tests. Genet. Psychol. Monogr. *14:* 1–92 (1933).

BAYLEY, N.: Comparisons of mental and motor test scores for ages 1–15 months by sex, birth order, race, geographical location and education of parents. Child Develop. *36:* 379–411 (1965).

BAYLEY, N.: The Bayley scales of infant development (Psychological Corp., New York 1969).

BAYLEY, N.: Development of mental abilities; in MUSSEN Carmichael's manual of child psychology, vol. 1 (Wiley, New York 1970).

BERLINER, D.C. and CAHEN, L.S.: Trait-treatment interactions and learning; to appear in KERLINGER Review of research in education, 1973 (Peacock, Itasca, in press, 1973).

BURT, C.; JONES, E.; MILLER, E., and MOODIE, W.: How the mind works (Appleton-Century-Crofts, New York 1934).

COLE, M.; GAY, J.; GLICK, J.A., and SHARP, D.W.: The cultural context of learning and thinking (Basic Books, New York 1971).

ESCALONA, S.K. and CORMAN, H.H.: The validation of Piaget's hypotheses concerning the development of sensori-motor intelligence. Methodological issues. Proc. Soc. Res. Child Develop. Meet. 1967.

GUILFORD, J.P.: Three faces of intellect. Amer. Psychol. *14:* 469–479 (1959).

HUNT, J. McV. and UZGIRIS, I.C.: Scales of perceptual cognitive development; unpubl. manuscript, University of Illinois (1966).

KING, W. and SEEGMILLER, B.: Cognitive development from 14 to 22 months of age in black, male, first-born infants assessed by the Bayley and Hunt-Uzgiris scales. Proc. Soc. Res. Child Develop. Meet., Minneapolis 1971.

LEWIS, M.: State as an infant-environment interaction. An analysis of mother-infant behavior as a function of sex. Merrill-Palmer Quart. *18:* 95–121 (1972).

LEWIS, M. and LEE-PAINTER, S.: An infant's interaction with its social world. The origin of meaning. Proc. Canad. Psychol. Ass. Meet., Symp. on parent-child observation studies and their problems. Montreal 1972.

LEWIS, M. and McGURK, H.: The evaluation of infant intelligence. Infant intelligence scores – true or false? Res. Bull. 72–32, Princeton, Educational Testing Service, 1972. Science (in press).

McCALL, R.B.; HOGARTY, P.S., and HURLBURT, N.: Transitions in infant sensorimotor development and the prediction of childhood IQ. Amer. Psychol. *27:* 728–748 (1972).

STOTT, L.H. and BALL, R.S.: Infant and preschool mental tests. Review and evaluation. Monogr. Soc. Res. in Child Develop., vol. *30:* serial No. 101 (1965).

THOMAS, H.: Psychological assessment instruments for use with human infants. Merrill-Palmer Quart. *16:* 179–224 (1970).

Request reprints from: Dr. MICHAEL LEWIS, Educational Testing Service, *Princeton, NJ 08540* (USA)

Human Develop. *16:* 119–132 (1973)

Disciplinary Barriers to Progress in Behavior Genetics: Defensive Reactions to Bits and Pieces[1]

M. F. Elias

West Virginia University, Morgantown, W. Va.

Abstract. The broad perspective provided by an interdisciplinary approach to behavior genetics seems essential for the synthesis of available data and the application of resulting generalizations to the needs of society. Such an approach has long been impeded by attempts to determine how much of a particular behavior is contributed by heredity and how much by environment. Contemporary behavior geneticists view this approach as meaningless and suggest that the appropriate question is how heredity and environment interact to influence behavior. Increased emphasis on the underlying mechanisms of environment-heredity interactions fosters interdisciplinary research by removing the need for extreme defensive reactions on behalf of either nature or nurture.

Key Words
Behavior genetics
Ideological bias
Eugenics
Environment
Early experience
Postnatal effects
Heredity

It has been argued [SEEMAN and MARKS, 1962] that an inverse relationship frequently exists between the degree to which research is relevant to the behavior of individuals and society and the extent to which it lends itself to methodological sophistication. Certainly, the questions raised by human behavior geneticists defy methodological precision, and their answers are profoundly important to the quality of human life. Yet the most severe limitations on the progress of behavior genetics are not necessarily methodological. Rather, they may be imposed by the emotional and ideological resistance which is inevitably directed toward research with highly visible implications for human beings.

[1] Many thanks are extended to Miss JUDITH L. HUFF, Department of Sociology and Center for the Study of Aging and Human Development, Duke University, Mrs. MARA SIMMERMAN, Center for the Study of Aging and Human Development, Duke University, and Miss JEANINE CARVER, Department of Psychology, University of North Carolina, for their assistance in the preparation of this manuscript.

Some Extreme Positions

BRESSLER [1968], ECKLAND [1967] and HALLER [1968] make a strong case that social scientists, particularly sociologists, have been traditionally reluctant to embrace biological and genetic approaches to the study of behavior. They all seem to agree that this reluctance is partially related to a vested interest in establishing a strong environmentalist approach, and that this emphasis on environment as opposed to heredity is rooted in traditionally liberal values. HALLER [1968] points out that this resistance to biogenetics is related to intellectual as well as ideological rejection of hereditary explanations. He points to the paucity of respectable human genetics research before 1920. HALLER notes that DAVENPORT [1912], the nation's most influential geneticist in the early 1900s, argued that many character traits had simple Mendelian explanations. Insanity, feeblemindedness, shyness, love of alcohol, mechanical ability, and shiftlessness were viewed as recessive, while violent temper and laziness were dominant.

Because of the disciplinary overlap between social psychology and sociology, association of the concepts of instinct and heredity at the hands of psychologist McDOUGALL [1908] may have contributed far more to intellectual rejection of behavior genetics than any of the misinformed and over-enthusiastic biologists cited by HALLER [1968]. In his immensely popular *Introduction to social psychology*, McDOUGALL [1908] developed the thesis that individuals and races differ in the strengths of a variety of instincts and inherited tendencies. He attempted to demonstrate that all social interaction is based on inherited instinctive action. As BORING [1950], points out, there is no end to the list of instincts that can be developed, and McDOUGALL's social psychology fell into scientific disrepute when psychologists discovered that anyone can make up his own list and that there is no way to prove that one list is more correct than another [BORING, 1950, p. 718]. But the damage was done. The concept of instinct was abused. Genetic determinants of behavior were confused with instinct, and the concepts of genetic predisposition and instinct were associated with the introspective method which was rejected by American psychologists and sociologists alike.

HALLER [1968, p. 217] points out that the academic assault against extreme hereditarian interpretations of human behavior did not begin much before 1920. He argues that the uncritical use of the Binet intelligence test in the early 1900s reinforced hereditarian extremism by providing 'conclusive proof that, except for Jews, those races that were believed to be inferior were in fact inferior' and that 'most criminals, prostitutes, tramps, and other undesirables were hereditary morons'. The result was a widespread concern with hereditarian reform which climaxed in the 1920's when the Congress of the United States enacted a law restricting immigration, particularly of groups assumed to be racially inferior [HIGAM, 1955]. It seems, from HALLER's account that a number of prestigious biologists and social scientists drew socially conservative conclusions from hereditarian interpretations of human behavior. For example, DAVENPORT [1912, p.281] advised a national conference of social workers that social reform was futile and the only way to secure innate capacity is by breeding it. McDOUGALL [1921] called for the replacement of democracy by a caste system based on biological capacity with legal restrictions upon breeding by the lower castes and upon breeding between the castes.

Assuming that social scientists are traditionally liberal and have a vested interest in a strong environmentalist approach [BRESSLER, 1968; ECKLAND, 1967; HALLER, 1968], it is not surprising that early opposition came from sociologists. WARD [1903] insisted that progress and the dissemination of technology and culture rather than biological selection explained the evolution of human society. BOAS [1911] argued that the lower classes did not differ from the upper classes in biological inheritance, but rather in their access to social heritage.

Arguments by WARD [1903] and BOAS [1911] represent extreme environmentalistic reactions to extreme hereditarian interpretations of behavior. Many contemporary sociologists and anthropologists [HALLER, 1968] recognize that biological selection has not creased but interacts with cultural and technological evolution in a reciprocal manner. Further, in human beings, assortative mating may come about by marriages between phenotypically similar, and presumably, genotypically similar individuals. Thus, while it is clear that upward mobility is restricted by a variety of environmental factors, the possibility that social classes may represent breeding populations cannot be ruled out.

WATSON's behaviorism represents an extreme environmentalist reaction within the field of psychology. 'I should like to go one step further now and say, give me a dozen healthy infants, well formed, and my own specified world to bring them up in and I'll guarantee to take any one at random and train him to become any type of specialist I might select – doctor, lawyer, artist, merchant-chief and, yes even beggerman and thief, regardless of his talents, penchants, tendencies, abilities, vocations and the race of his ancestors' [WATSON, 1930, p. 104].

WATSON [1930], and more recently, SKINNER [1969] emphasize the fact that the statement goes beyond its facts to counteract extreme hereditarian views that had existed for centuries, and to emphasize what could be done despite genetic limitations. Extreme views in one direction may be necessary to exert sufficient counterforce to extreme views in another. However, the pervasive influence of behaviorism on American psychology, potentiated by functionalism and the American *Zeitgeist* which was against hereditary right and for the recognition of personal achievement [BORING, 1950, pp. 507–508], resulted in an overemphasis on environment and an unfortunate neglect of genetic factors in behavior during the early years when the character of American psychology was being established.

Ideological Biases

In addition to the slowing of the development of behavior genetics which resulted from extreme hereditarian positions countered by extreme environmentalist reactions, there have been unfortunate associations of genetics and political ideology which may well have resulted in an irrational aversion to the association of the words 'behavior' and 'genetics'. A good example is provided by the incorporation of pseudogenetic arguments into the Nazi doctrines of the 1930's. Although the International Genetics Congress took an official stand against the scientific validity of these doctrines [BENEDICT, 1940, pp. 259–266], association of the concept of hereditary predisposition with a repugnant ideology must have reinforced the strong environmental position shared by many social scientists. BRESSLER [1968, p. 180] makes this point very well in his chapter in *Genetics,* where he points out that: 'The sociological aversion to social biology, however, is based on more than a routine rejection of faulty evidence. It is fortified by the lingering suspicion that an explanatory sequence that begins with the organism inevitably ends with predatory ethics.'

Unfortunate association of the concepts of genetics and ideological bias are not relegated to the distant past. Those who disagree may find GEORGE's report [1962] to the Governor of Alabama of particular interest. Fortunately, obvious selection of data to legitimize social ideologies [GEORGE, 1962] are not given serious attention by intelligent men. Unfortunately, for the much needed rapproachment between social sciences and biogenetics, ethical, though possibly unpopular, positions are often distorted by other authors who wish to claim support for their thesis. Examples of such distortion may be found in a recent paper by McCONNELL [1970].

McCONNELL [1970, p. 904], a biophysicist, argues that 'our present in-cipient social breakdown is related to spiritual decay and insufficient intel-ligence to match the growing complexities of civilization'. He argues for a selective breeding program for intelligence which he perceives as an im-portant aspect of 'genetic fitness'. 'Would it be immoral to disregard eugenic considerations while attempting to control man's numbers? The question might be approached by a homely example from applied biology. Suppose a farmer had a herd of cows that was too big for his pasture. Would he reduce the herd at random or would he remove the less fit? ... There seems to be no moral reason why we should not encourage genetic fitness' [McCONNELL, 1970, p. 903].

A number of serious objections can be raised to a eugenics program which features selection for intelligence as a means of improving fitness. Knowl-edge of human genetics has not reached a point where objective decisions can be made with regard to those qualities which a fit man must possess. If anything, evidence has pointed to the fact that a diversity of characteristics, rather than extremes of certain characteristics, have survival value for the organism; and that those sets of characteristics which are most suitable for survival in a particular environment will evolve naturally [DOBZHANSKY, 1967]. Further, eugenics programs which emphasize alterations of breeding patterns ignore the growing behavioral genetics literature which indicates that phenotype may be modified, sometimes drastically, by the environment in which it exists. Thus improving environmental conditions for all persons becomes a legitimate approach to eugenics, both in the sense of immediate improvement in society and improvement in future generations. Exclusively hereditarian concepts of eugenics may stem from its earliest conception by GALTON [1869] as a means of improving fitness of the human race by selective breeding for superior persons. The fundamental problem in GALTON's time, and now, is that there is by no means agreement with regard to those characteristics which a 'superior' person must possess. Further, there are, as the papers in this symposium indicate, many who disagree with an approach to improving society which is based on a striving to ensure that all men are within the limits of a standard norm.

The most damaging aspect of the paper with regard to reinforcement of fears concerning the predatory nature of human behavior genetic research is not, however, his eugenics thesis *per se,* but the fact that McCONNELL [1970] distorts JENSEN's argument to reinforce this thesis. McCONNELL [1970, p. 904] asks: 'Is selective breeding for intelligence practical?' He answers: 'Yes beyond a shadow of a doubt, as shown by JENSEN's paper.'

JENSEN has indeed concluded that evidence for mean differences between Negro and white intelligence is less consistent with an environmental hypothesis than with a genetic hypothesis. However, at no point in his papers does JENSEN [1969, 1970] defend a program of selection for intelligence. Regardless of the variety of objections [BODMER and CAVALLI-SFORZA, 1970; LEWONTIN, 1970] that can be raised with regard to his conclusions, the appeal is for consideration of the possible contribution of genotype to individual differences, and this appeal is made in light of a need for improved educational programs for the intellectually disadvantaged.

It is essential that scientists defend society against the misuses of scientific evidence for political and social ends, but overreaction, as in the past, may limit the usefulness of behavior genetics to society by discrediting the validity of the question as well as the correctness of the answer. BODMER and CAVALLI-SFORZA's [1970] response to JENSEN's paper provides an example. These investigators point to the fundamental weakness in JENSEN's genetic hypothesis, i.e. it is based on the erroneous assumption that high heritability of intelligence within the white population indicates that genetic factors are strongly implicated in mean differences in IQ between Negroes and whites. They indicate, quite appropriately, that a proper approach to the study of the basis for mean IQ differences between Negroes and whites is by means of cross fostering designs applied sufficiently early in life so as to minimize environmental differences. However, they prejudge the outcome of the research and forbid its execution because of possible social implications. In the very same paper they acknowledge the inherent dangers in the control of scientific inquiry.

Certainly, vigorous responses to JENSEN's [1969, 1970] papers which question either the scientific validity of his conclusions or their implications for social and political action should be encouraged. However, it seems that the two issues should be clearly separated so that the validity of the genetic hypothesis is not decided on the basis of its social and political implications. This does not imply that the question of political and social implications should not be subjected to careful examination. On the contrary, the increasing relevance of findings in behavior genetics for social action, e.g., population control, genetic counseling, genetic intervention, educational programs and legislation, demands an increasingly intelligent participation of political scientists, sociologists, and educational and social scientists in interdisciplinary behavior genetic research projects.

Interdisciplinary projects could provide protection against the misuses of genetic findings by those biologists who lack the skill necessary to examine the broad implications of their research. At the same time social scientists could be brought in contact with a representative sampling of the behavior genetics research literature. Areas of behavior genetic research that invite scientific and ideological reaction by virtue of the questions raised, e.g. JENSEN [1969], appear to receive much wider publicity than areas with less apparent but equally strong implications for social action. Consequently, social scientists who are isolated by disciplinary boundaries may be more likely to come into contact with areas of behavior genetic research that are criticized by the biological community. This selected exposure to a controversial literature may serve to reinforce the tendency on the part of many social scientists to regard all areas of behavior genetic investigation with suspicion.

The Search for 'How'

The controversial literature in behavior genetics seems to involve attempts to determine the proportional contribution of heredity and environment to a particular behavioral trait. Many contemporary behavior geneticists [DOBZHANSKY, 1967; GOTTESMAN, 1968; THODAY and PARKES, 1968; THOMPSON, 1968; VANDENBERG, 1968 a, b] argue that such attempts are futile because they make the erroneous assumption that heredity and environment combine in a static, additive fashion. These investigators view human and animal behavior as a process of constant change in which genes and environment are components of a reciprocal feedback system. Thus, the proportional contribution of heredity to the variance of a given trait varies under different environmental conditions. Similarly, under different hereditary conditions, the relative contributions of various environments will differ. This emphasis on the interaction of heredity and environment is not inconsistent with dialectic psychology [PAYNE, 1968] which considers the organism and the environment as active participants in the process of change.

Behavior geneticists who emphasize the interaction of heredity and environment point out that only genes can be inherited. Since their influence on behavior is always thus indirect, a proper task for the behavior geneticists is to ask how, rather than how much, heredity and environment influence behavior. ANASTASI [1958] has provided an excellent argument for the study of how. She indicates that many intervening mechanisms, varying from those which are close to direct gene action to those which exert a more direct influence on environment, may be studied. In the present paper, studies of how heredity and environment influence behavior have been arbitrarily divided into two levels: the molecular and the molar. The bulk of the work in behavior genetics has been done at the molecular level. The molar level builds on end points of study at the molecular level. Each approach deals with variables located somewhere along a continuum of closeness either to gene action or environment, but each emphasizes the interaction of environment and heredity. Thus, neither approach forces investigators to take a defensive posture on the side of either nature or nurture. The extensive literature with regard to these two levels of investigation cannot be reviewed here. However, several examples will be provided in order to emphasize the importance of environment in modern behavior genetics.

Molecular behavior genetics. Investigations at the molecular level [FULLER, 1956; MERRELL, 1965; THIESSEN, 1971] search for the relationship between behavior and one or several genes. They trace the pathways of expression between these genes and corresponding behavior by examining 'path markers', e.g., neurons, hormones, and enzymes. 'Molecular' animal research has concentrated on seizure susceptibility, alcohol preference and aversion, and the biochemical basis of cognitive and emotional behavior [LINDZEY *et al.,* 1971; MCCLEARN, 1971]. Much human research has focused on metabolic disorders, particularly those associated with mental retardation. These studies have lead to the treatment of phenolketonuria with dietary supplement [ANDERSON and SIEGEL, 1968] and may eventually lead to enzyme replacement therapy [PORTER *et al.,* 1971] for such diseases as metachromatic leukodystrophy.

Research at the molecular level also includes cytogenetic studies. Studies by JARVIK and her colleagues are particularly important to the development of a life-span approach to behavior genetics. These investigators [BETTNER *et al.,* 1971; JARVIK *et al.,* 1962; JARVIK, 1969; JARVIK and KATO, 1970] are concerned with the relationship between chromosome loss, psychopathology, aging, and senile dementia.

Dramatic evidence for the modifiability of genetically influenced phenotype characteristics by environment is provided by studies at the molecular level. The biochemical and structural characteristics which have been identified as mediators between genes and behavior have been modified by enriched or deprived social environments. Systematic manipulation of these environments in studies with small animals have revealed increased size and biochemical (enzymatic) changes in the developing brain and the adult brain [DAS and ALTMAN, 1966; ROSENZWEIG, 1969].

Molar behavior genetics. Physical and behavioral characteristics which may serve as an end point for the more molecularly oriented investigations may serve as intervening mechanisms at the molar level of investigation. Here, the search for intervening mechanisms can include studies of the influence of health, body build, skin color, nutrition, social class membership, language skills, education and cultural heritage on the interaction of heredity and environment as they jointly affect behavior. Early experience studies and studies of prenatal determinants of behavior provide excellent examples of the kinds of molar research which provide a basis for building interdisciplinary approaches to behavior genetics.

Early experience studies remove disciplinary barriers by including both genetic and environmental variables in the same design. They do so by either manipulating genotype and environment in the same study or by exploring the effect of environmental conditions on behavior which is assumed, or proven, to be strongly influenced by genotype. These studies explore the range of variation in this behavior which may be induced by environmental manipulations at various stages of development. The very fact that these studies do not deny the importance of heredity has enabled them to provide strong support for the social scientist's argument for the importance of environment. The importance of genotype or environment cannot be demonstrated in an experiment which does not manipulate both.

Early experience research, including studies with humans featuring investigations of child rearing practices, e.g., MILNER [1951], have been reviewed by ANASTASI [1958], among many others. However, a review chapter by DENENBERG [1969] is worth noting because he has done an excellent job of synthesizing the findings for a variety of species, i.e., dogs, mice, rats, monkeys, and man. The experimental treatments were the nature of mothering, maternal deprivation, peer deprivation, stress and restricted environment. All of these treatments were not applied to each of these species, and the behavioral measures (aggression, problem solving, pain perception, sexual behavior, maternal behavior, height of adult males, and the onset of menarche) were not always identical. However, they all had an important element in common, i.e. a strong genetic base and/or adaptive value in the evolutionary sense of aiding in survival of the organism. Nevertheless, they were drastically modified by manipulation of early postnatal experience. Further, in all animals studied, modifications in behavior lasted well into maturity. For rats, the effects not only lasted into old age but were observed for both the offspring and the grandchildren of the experimental animals. For each of the species studied, the number of behaviors affected and the direction and persistence of the behavioral modification were all determined by the age of the animal at the time of treatment.

Research on prenatal determinants of behavior indicates that hereditary and environmental factors co-vary from the moment of conception. Joffe [1969] has presented an extensive survey of this work. Again, a majority of studies have been done with animals because of the difficulty in obtaining sufficient control over genetic and postnatal environmental variables with human subjects. Animal studies clearly indicate that exposure to X-rays, drugs, sex hormones and stress during pregnancy can have a deleterious effect on the emotional and/or cognitive behavior of the offspring. Yet, aside from clinical reports, Joffe [1969] found a limited number of studies which explored the relation of these variables to behavior in human children. For example, there seems to be a wealth of evidence [Montagu, 1962] indicating that malnutrition during pregnancy has teratogenic effects on the developing nervous system in humans. Yet Joffe [1969] could find only one experimental investigation of the effects of maternal nutrition during pregnancy on the behavior of children. Harrell et al. [1955] found that mean IQ of children of three groups of mothers given three different vitamin supplements was significantly higher, in a statistical sense, than mean IQ of the children of mothers that received a placebo. In a Virginia clinic, the mean IQ of the progeny of the three vitamin supplement groups combined was 3.7 IQ points higher than the placebo group at the age of three, and 5.2 points higher at the age of four. These results were not replicated in a Kentucky clinic, but the investigators argue that the nutrition of these mothers was adequate without vitamin supplement.

These studies of early experience and prenatal environment invite increased participation by social scientists in behavior genetics research. They place an emphasis on the importance of environment, they are relevant to social theory, and if nothing else, knowledge of this literature is necessary for intelligent criticism of behavior genetics research which deals with how much rather than how. For example, early experience findings and prenatal data are particularly relevant to the current nature-nurture controversy which is focused on the question of a genetic basis for differences in intellectual functioning between Negroes and whites.[2] These studies indicate that

---

[2] Pasamanick et al. [1956] examined the records of large samples of Negroes and whites in Baltimore and found a higher frequency of a variety of medical complication of pregnancy, including deficiencies in maternal diet, in lower than higher socioeconomic groups, and a higher frequency among Negroes than among whites.

phenotype may be altered, in some cases drastically, by very early environmental conditions. They do not argue against the very strong evidence for the high heritability of intelligence for a particular population under given environmental conditions [BURT, 1972; ERLENMEYER-KEMLING and JARVIK, 1963; SCHULL and NEEL, 1965]. Neither do they suggest that traits influenced by genes are infinitely modifiable by training or manipulation of the environment. Such a conclusion is the kind of wishful thinking that has perpetuated the nature-nurture controversy. However, these data do justify serious questioning of the thesis that mean differences in IQ between Negroes and whites are more strongly related to genotype than they are to environmental differences between the two populations. This generalization can only be validated by a demonstration of differences in intellectual functioning between these two populations under conditions in which environmental influences are uniform. Since this degree of control over environmental factors is very difficult to achieve with humans, differences in intellectual functioning among individuals and between groups must be attributed to some interactive combination of hereditary and environmental factors.

The literature on prenatal determinants of behavior emphasizes the methodological difficulties encountered when attempts are made to separate these interacting factors. Even if it were possible to employ experimental designs in which Negro and white children, or children from different social classes were cross-fostered immediately after birth, the correlation between heredity and environmental factors, which begins at conception, could not be eliminated. Thus, it appears that the traditional question of the proportional contribution of heredity and environment is indeed unanswerable. Moreover, it seems to have established barriers to interdisciplinary research in behavior genetics by forcing disciplines with a vested interest in either nature or nurture to take sides.

The assumption in this paper has been that interdisciplinary studies can enhance the contribution of behavior genetic research to the problems facing society. It might be argued that research in the areas previously discussed, i.e. molar and the molecular behavioral genetics, is already going on within disciplines, and that an appreciable increase in data would not be realized by encouraging social, behavioral, and biological scientists to exchange information and to engage in cooperative research projects. This may be true, however, accumulation of data is not the exclusive goal of scientific inquiry. RIEGEL [1971] has emphasized the fact that scientific inquiry must go beyond the accumulation of isolated bits and pieces of data. He does not deny the importance of data collection. Rather he notes that we already have an information overload in many disciplines such as psychology, and that what is needed is increased effort to synthesize and organize existing data. It seems that cooperative efforts across disciplines are essential if this kind of synthesis is to be accomplished for behavior genetics.

Efforts toward interdisciplinary approaches to behavior genetics are under way in the form of institutes (e.g. Institute for Behavior Genetics, University of Colorado), interdisciplinary departments (e.g. Department of Biobehavioral Sciences, University of Connecticut), and a variety of integrative books and papers [ANASTASI, 1958; GLASS, 1968; LERNER, 1968; LINDZEY et al., 1971; McCLEARN, 1971; VANDENBERG, 1968a, b]. However, these efforts must increase if we are to keep abreast of the bits and pieces which have grown at an enormous rate since the renaissance of interest in behavior genetics in the 1950's.

References

ANASTASI, A.: Heredity, environment, and the question'how?' Psychol. Rev. 65: 197–208 (1958).
ANDERSON, E. and SIEGEL, F.: Studies of behavior in genetically defined syndromes in man; in VANDENBERG Progress in human behavior genetics, pp. 7–15 (Johns Hopkins Press, Baltimore 1968).
BENEDICT, R.: Race. Science and politics (Modern Age Books, New York 1940).
BETTNER, L.G.; JARVIK, L.G., and BLUM, J.E.: Stroop color-word test, non-psychotic organic brain syndrome, and chromosome loss in aged twins. J. Geront. 26: 458–469 (1971).
BOAS, F.: The mind of primitive man (Macmillan, New York 1911).
BODMER, W.F. and CAVALLI-SFORZA, L.L.: Intelligence and race. Sci. Amer. 223: 19–29 (1970).
BORING, E.G.: A history of experimental psychology (Appleton Century Crofts, New York 1950).
BRESSLER, M.: Sociology, biology, and ideology; in GLASS Genetics, pp. 178–209 (Rockefeller University Press, New York 1968).
BURT, C.: Inheritance of general intelligence. Amer. Psychol. 27: 175–190 (1972).
DAS, G.D. and ALTMAN, J.: Behavioral manipulations and protein metabolism of the brain. Effects of restricted and enriched environments on the utilization of leucine ³H. Physiol. Behav. 1: 109–110 (1966).
DAVENPORT, C.B.: Heredity in relation to eugenics (Holt, New York 1911).
DAVENPORT, C.B.: Eugenics and charity. Proc. 39th Nat. Conf. Charities and Corrections, 1912; cited by HALLER [1968].
DENENBERG, V.H.: Animal studies of early experience. Some principles which have implications for human development; in HILL Minnesota symposia on child psychology, pp. 31–45 (University of Minnesota Press, Minneapolis 1969).
DOBZHANSKY, T.: Of flies and men. Amer. Psychol. 22: 41–48 (1967).

ECKLAND, B.K.: Genetics and sociology. A reconsideration. Amer. sociol. Rev. *32:* 173–194 (1967).

ERLENMEYER-KIMLING, L. and JARVIK, L.F.: Genetics and intelligence. A review. Science *142:* 1477–1479 (1963).

FULLER, J.L.: The path between genes and behavior characteristics. Eugen. Quart. *3:* 209–212 (1956).

GALTON, F.: Hereditary genius. An inquiry into its laws and consequences (Macmillan, London 1869).

GEORGE, W.C.: The biology of the race problem (National Putman Letters Committee, New York 1962).

GLASS, D.C. (ed.): Genetics (Rockefeller University Press, New York 1968).

GOTTESMAN, I.I.: Beyond the fringe-personality and psychopathology; in GLASS Genetics, pp. 59–68 (Rockefeller University Press, New York 1968).

HALLER, M.H.: Social sciences and genetics. A historical perspective; in GLASS Genetics, pp. 215–225 (Rockefeller University Press, New York 1968).

HARRELL, R.F.; WOODYARD, E., and GATES, A.E.: The effects of mother's diets on the intelligence of offspring. A study of the influence of vitamin supplementation on the diets of pregnant and lactating women on the intelligence of their children (Teachers College, Columbia University, New York 1955).

HIGAM, J.: Strangers in the land. Patterns of American nativism, 1860–1925 (Rutgers University Press, New Brunswick 1955).

JARVIK, L.F.: Cytogenetic aspects of psychopathology; in ZUBIN and SHAGASS Neurobiological aspects of psychopathology, pp. 266–280 (Grune & Stratton, New York 1969).

JARVIK, L.F.; KALLMANN, F.J., and FALEK, A.: Psychiatric genetics and aging. Gerontologist *2:* 164–166 (1962).

JARVIK, L.F. and KATO, T.: Chromosome examinations in aged twins. Amer. J. hum. Genet. *22:* 562–573 (1970).

JENSEN, A.R.: How much can we boost IQ and scholastic achievement? Harvard Educat. Rev. *39:* 1–123 (1969).

JENSEN, A.R.: Race and the genetics of intelligence. A reply to Lewontin. Bull. atomic Sci. *26:* 17–23 (1970).

JOFFE, J.M.: Prenatal determinantes of behavior (Pergamon, New York 1969).

LERNER, I.M.: Heredity, evolution, and society (Freeman, San Francisco 1968).

LEWONTIN, R.C.: Race and intelligence. Bull. atomic Sci. *26:* 2–8 (1970).

LINDZEY, G.; LOEHLIN, J.; MANOSEVITZ, M., and THIESSEN, D.: Behavioral genetics. Ann. Rev. Psychol. *22:* 39–94 (1971).

McCLEARN, G.M.: Behavioral genetics. Behav. Sci. *16:* 64–81 (1971).

McCONNELL, R.A.: The future revisited. Bio. Sci. *20:* 903–904 (1970).

McDOUGALL, W.: Introduction to social psychology (Luce, Boston 1908).

McDOUGALL, W.: Is America safe for democracy? (Scribers, New York 1921).

MERRELL, D.J.: Methodology in behavior genetics. J. Hered. *56:* 262–266 (1965).

MILNER, E.A.: A study of the relationships between reading readiness in grade one school children and patterns of parent-child interactions. Child Develop. *22:* 95–112 (1951).

MONTAGU, M.F.A.: Prenatal influences (Thomas, Springfield 1962).

PASAMANICK, B.; KNOBLOCH, H., and LILIENFELD, A.M.: Socioeconomic status and some precursors of neuropsychiatric disorder. Amer. J. Orthopsychiat. *26:* 594–601 (1956).

PAYNE, T.R.: S.L. Rubinstein and the philosophical foundations of Soviet psychology (Humanities Press, New York 1968).

PORTER, M.T.; FLUHARTY, A.L., and KIHARA, H.: Enzyme replacement therapy. A test tube cure for genetic disorders. Calif. ment. Hlth Res. Dig. *9:* 3–9 (1971).

RIEGEL, K.F.: On the history of psychological gerontology; in EISDORFER and LAWTON APA task force on aging (Amer. Psychol. Ass., Washington, in press, 1971).

ROSENZWEIG, M.R.: Environmental complexity, cerebral change, and behavior; in ENDLER, BOULTER, and OSSLER Contemporarv issues in developmental psychology, pp. 62–77 (Winston, New York 1969).

SCHULL, W.J. and NEEL, J.V.: The effects of inbreeding on Japanese children (Harper and Row, New York 1965).

SEEMAN, W. and MARKS, P.: The behavior of the psychologist at a choice point. Amer. Sci. *50:* 538–547 (1962).

SKINNER, B.F.: The phylogeny and ontogeny of behavior; in ENDLER, BOULTER, and OSSLER Contemporary issues in developmental psychology, pp. 62–75 (Holt, Rinehart, & Winston, New York 1969).

THIESSEN, D.D.: Reply to Wilcock on gene action and behavior. Psychol. Bull. *75:* 103–105 (1971).

THODAY, J.M. and PARKES, A.S.: Genetic and environmental influences on behavior (Plenum, New York 1968).

THOMPSON W.R.: Genetics and social behavior; in GLASS Genetics, pp. 79–101 (Rockefeller University Press, New York 1968).

VANDENBERG, S.G.: Nature and nurture of intelligence; in GLASS Genetics, pp. 3–68 (Rockefeller University Press, New York 1968a).

VANDENBERG, S.G.: Progress in human behavior genetics (Johns Hopkins Press, Baltimore (1968b).

WARD, L.F.: Pure sociology (Macmillan, New York 1903).

WATSON, J.B.: Behaviorism (Morton, New York 1930).

BF431 .I526   c.1
                                        100105 000
Intelligence : alter   vie

3 9310 00033703 8
GOSHEN COLLEGE-GOOD LIBRARY

WITHDRAWN

Request reprints from: Dr. MERRILL F. ELIAS, Department of Psychology, Syracuse University, *Syracuse NY 13210* (USA)